Winter Time Coloring Book
For Kids And Family

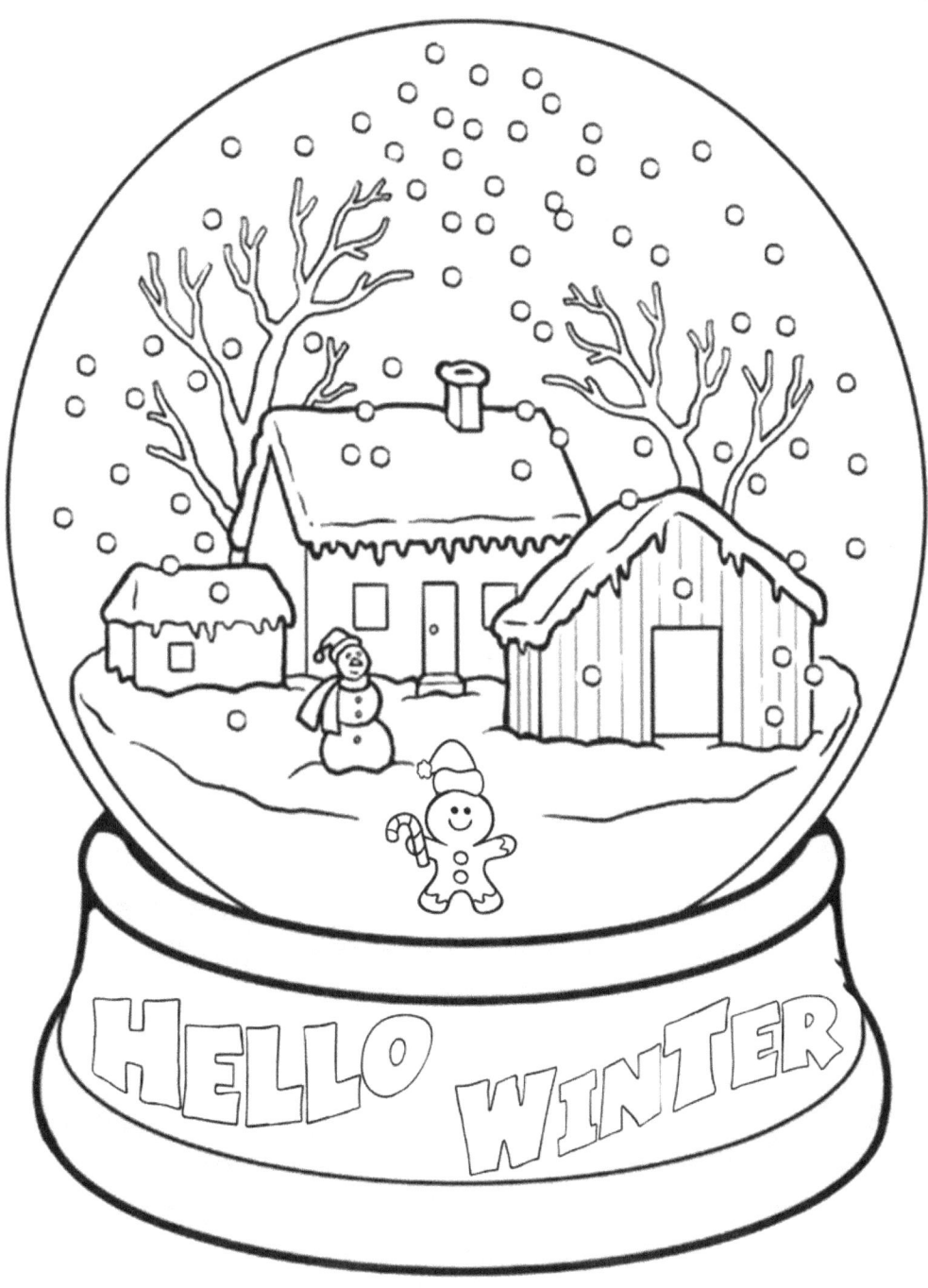

Nina Watson

Winter Time Coloring Book
For Kids and Family

Copyright: Published in the United States by **Nina.Watson**
Published November 2017

ISBN-13: 978-1981108213

ISBN-10: 1981108211

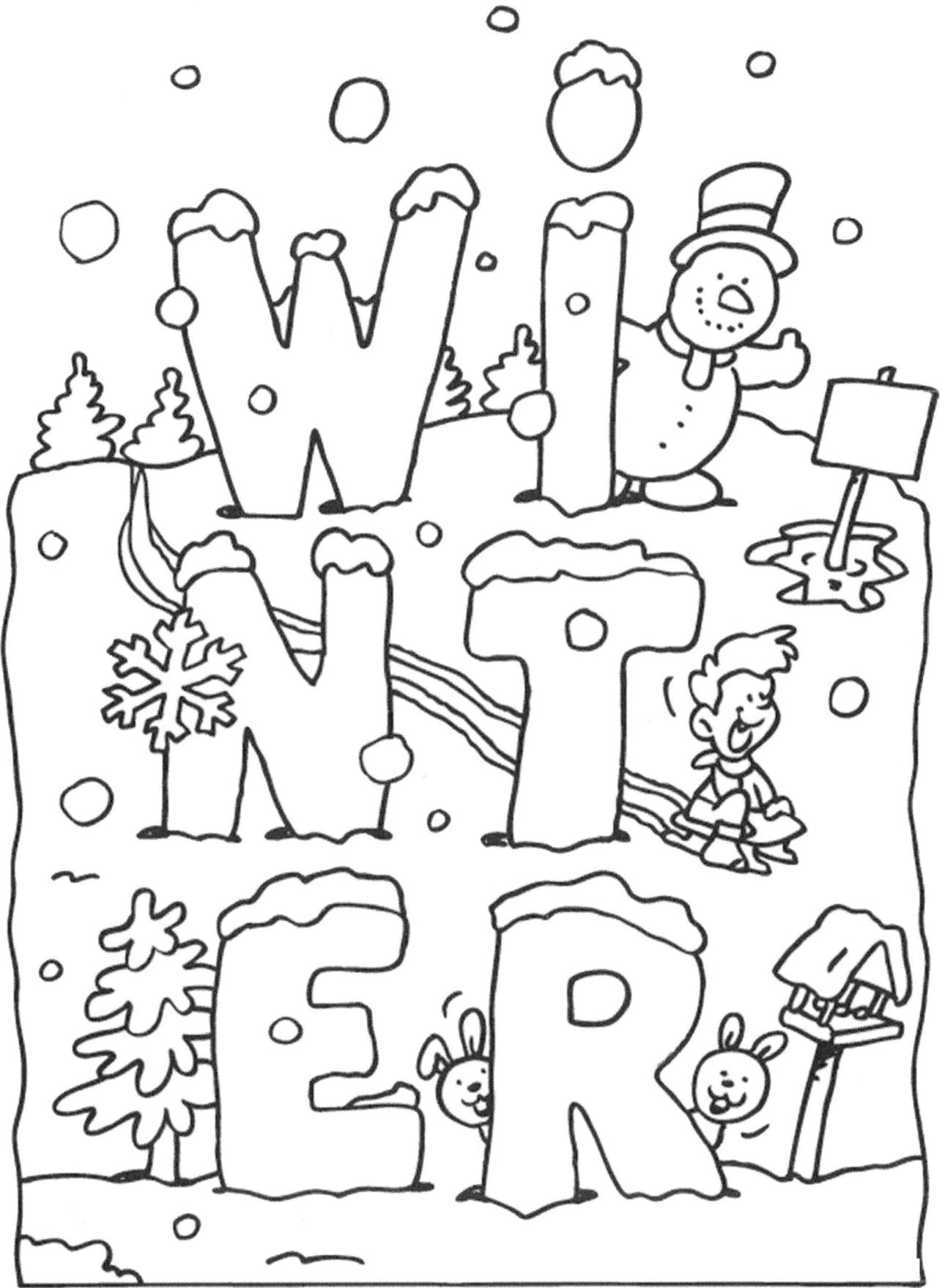

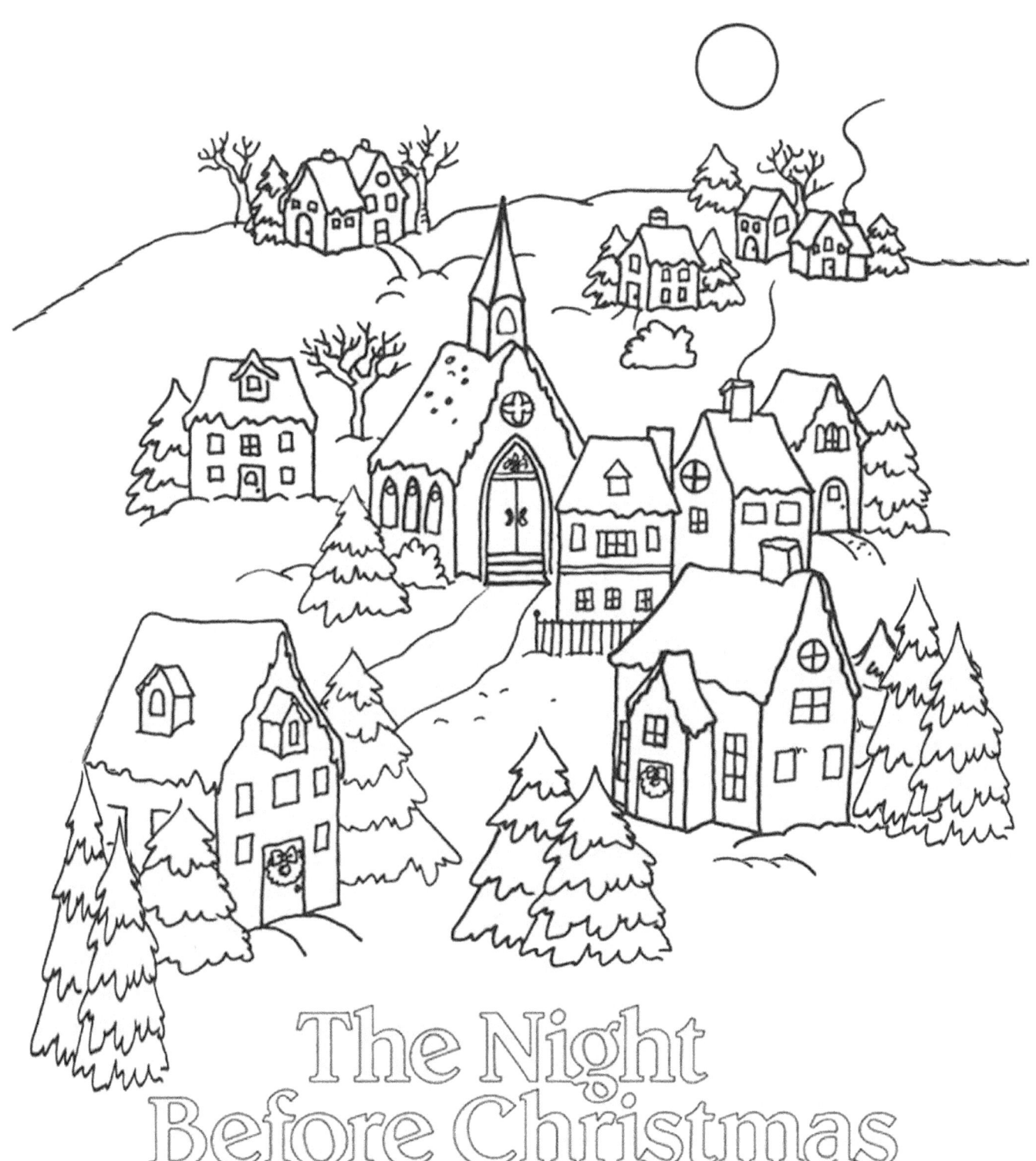

The Night
Before Christmas

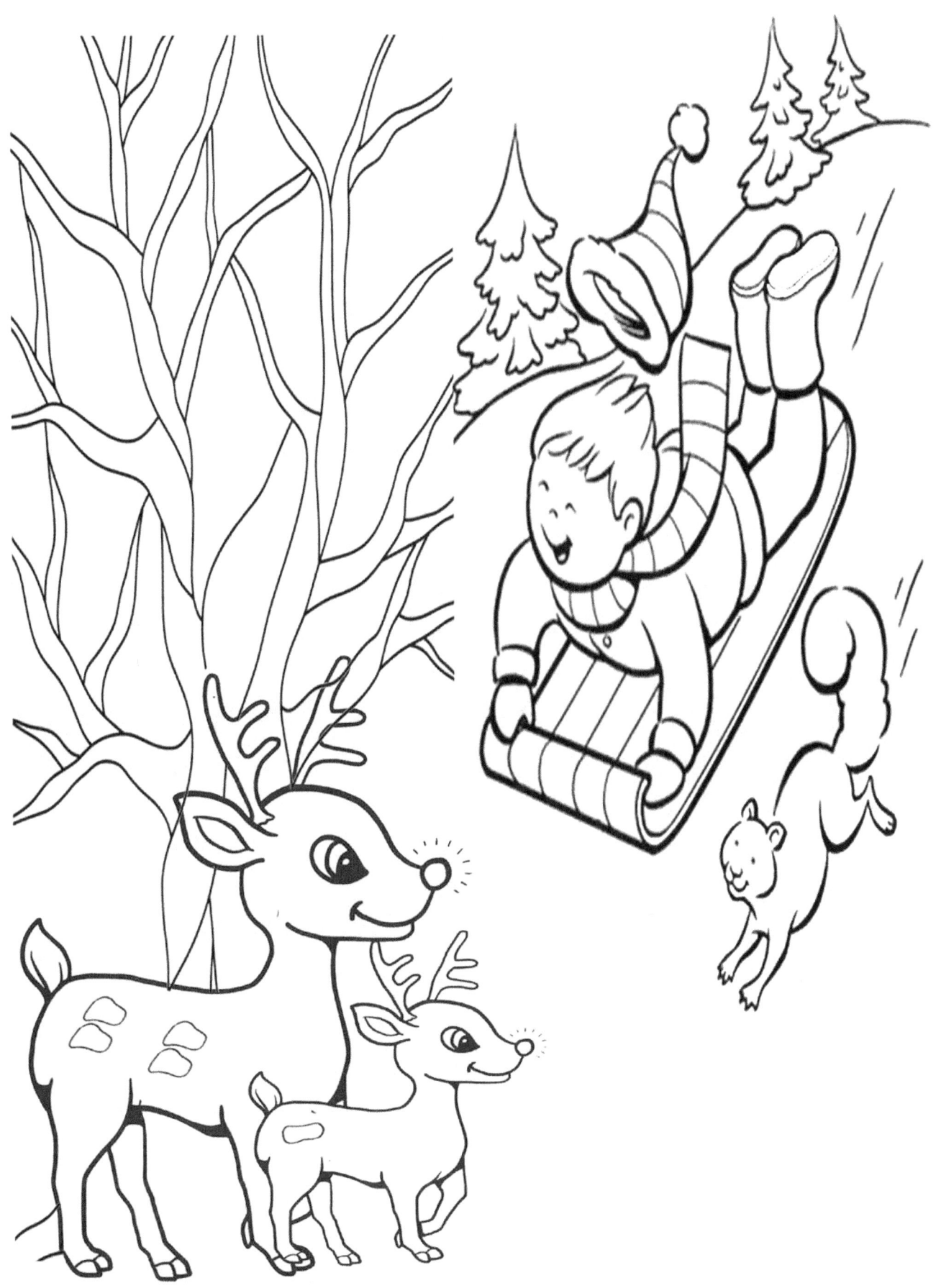

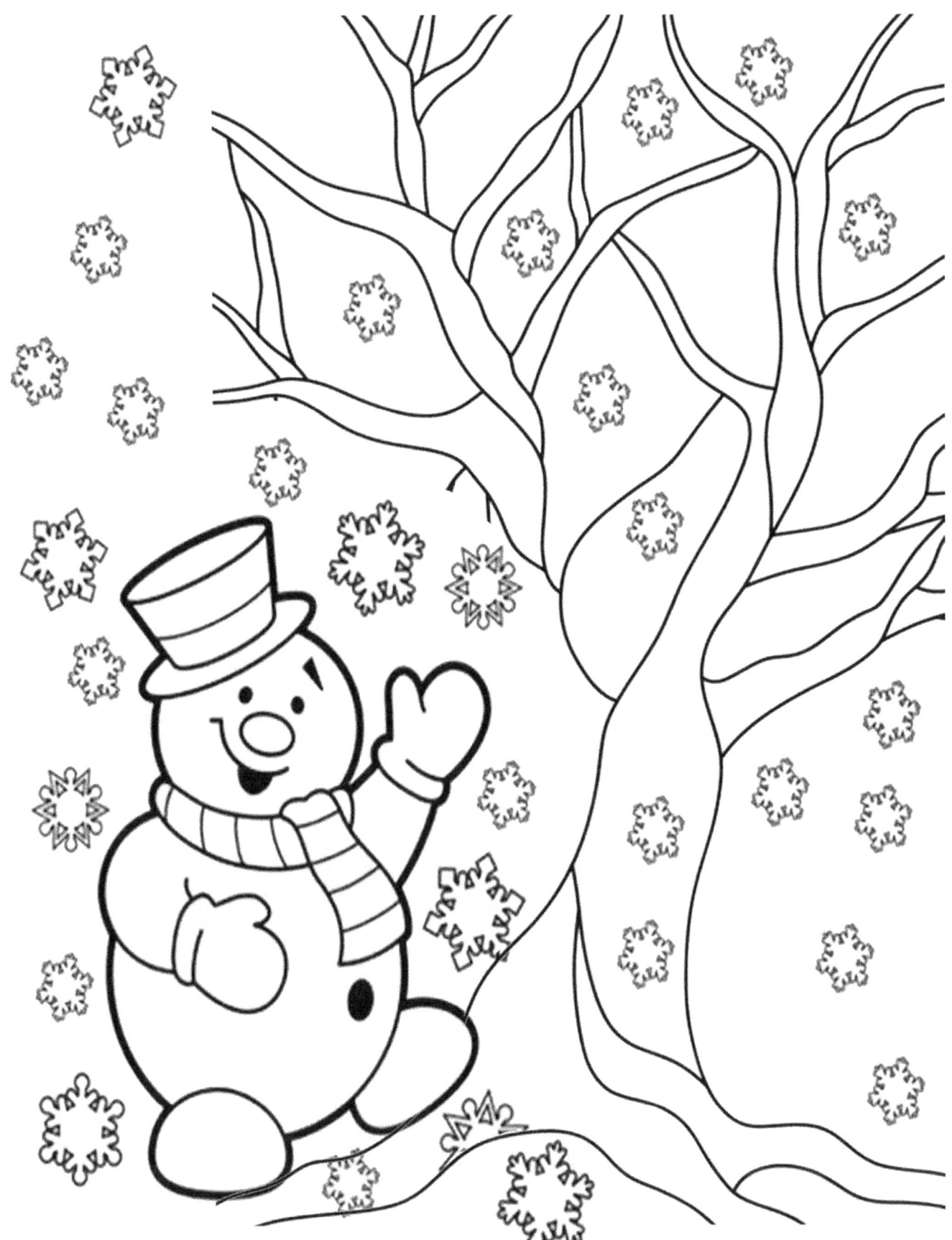

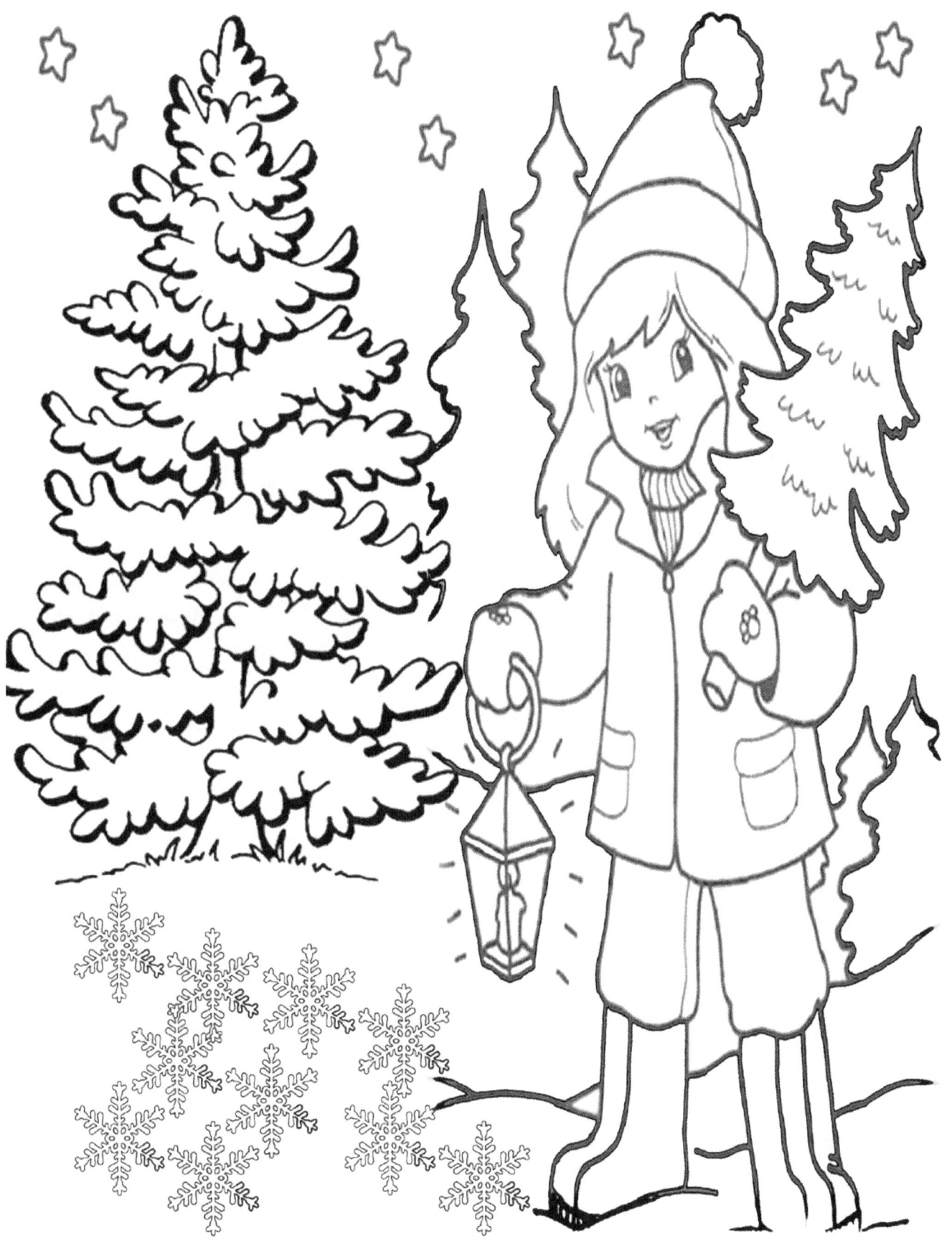

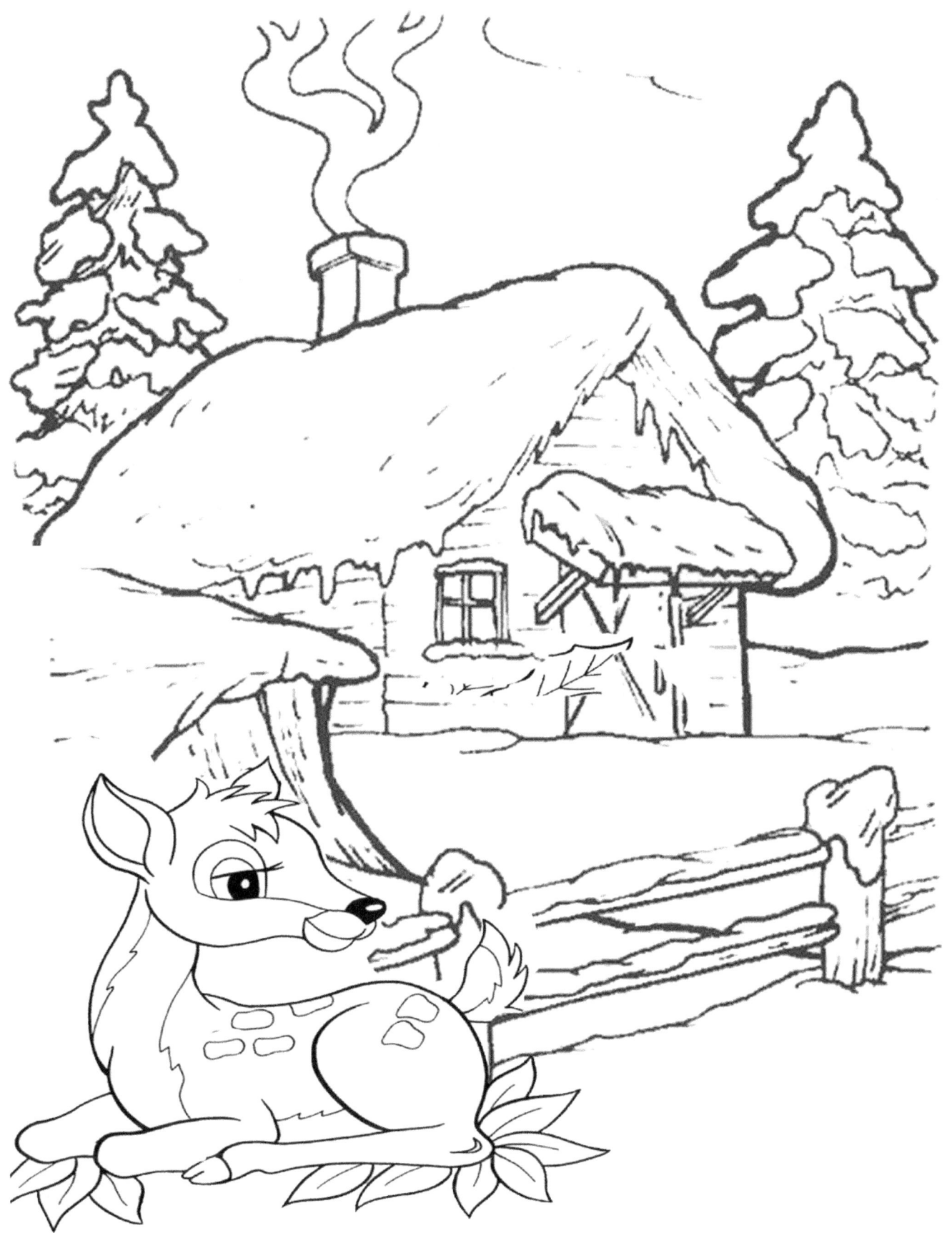

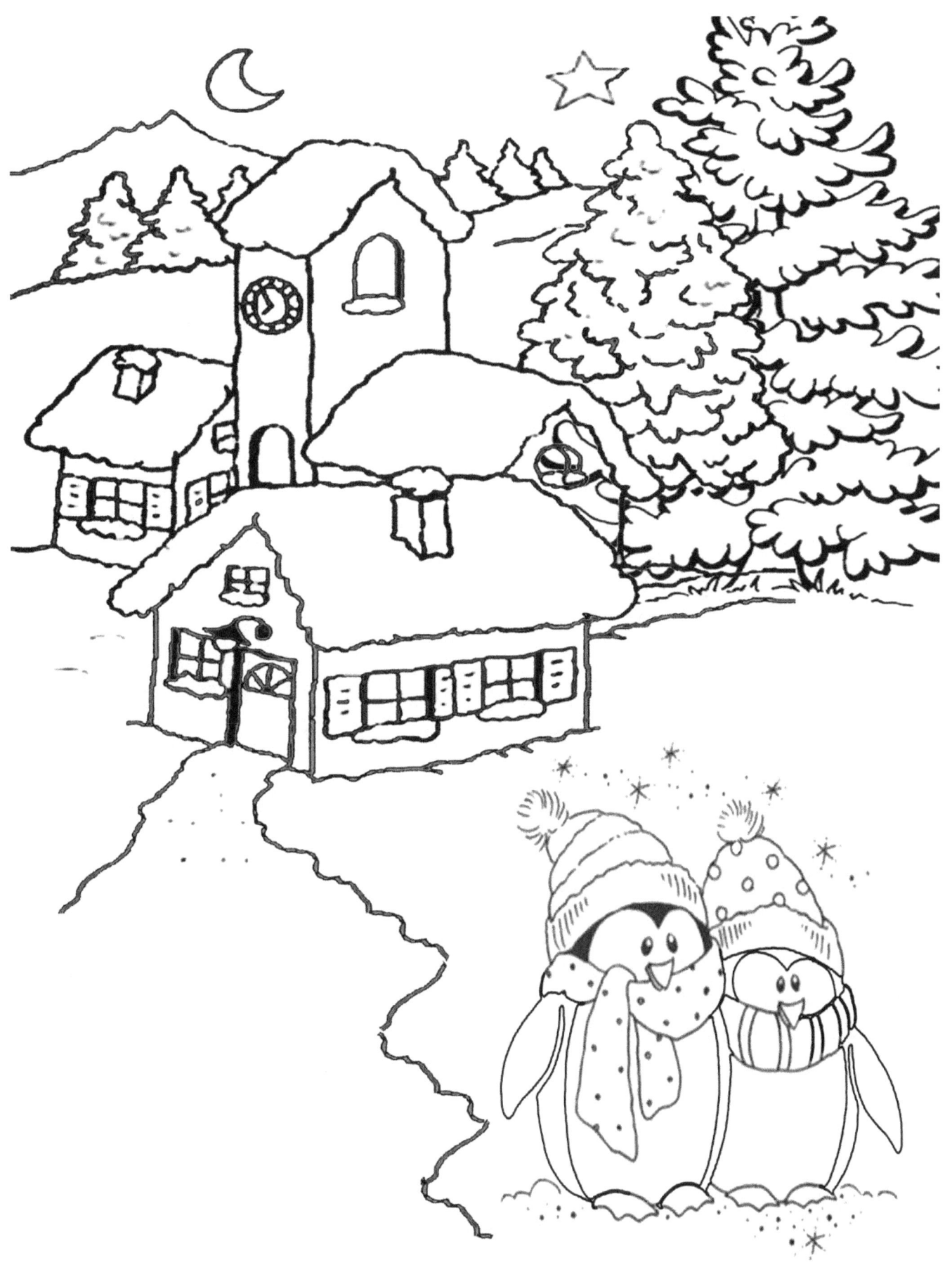

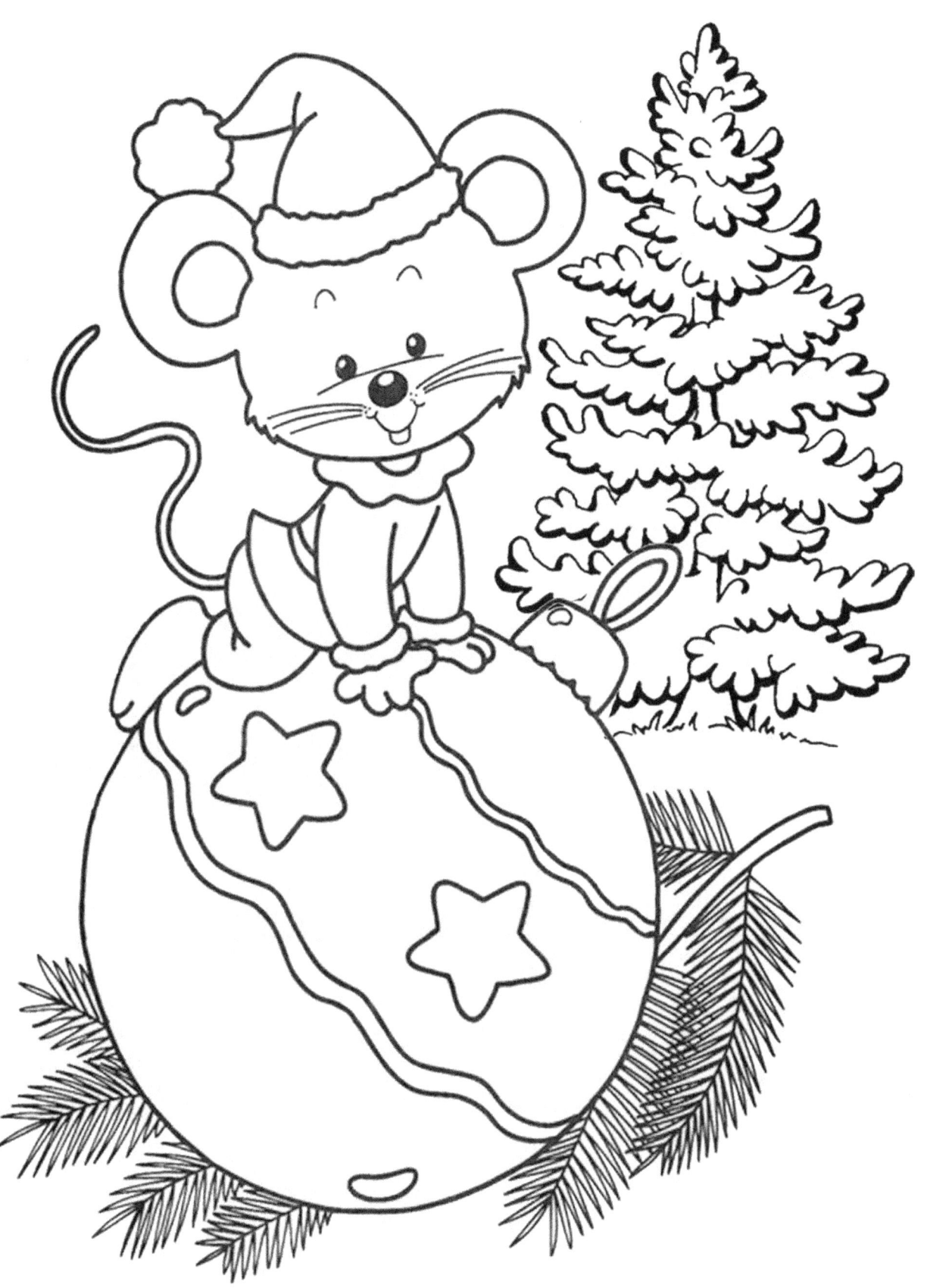

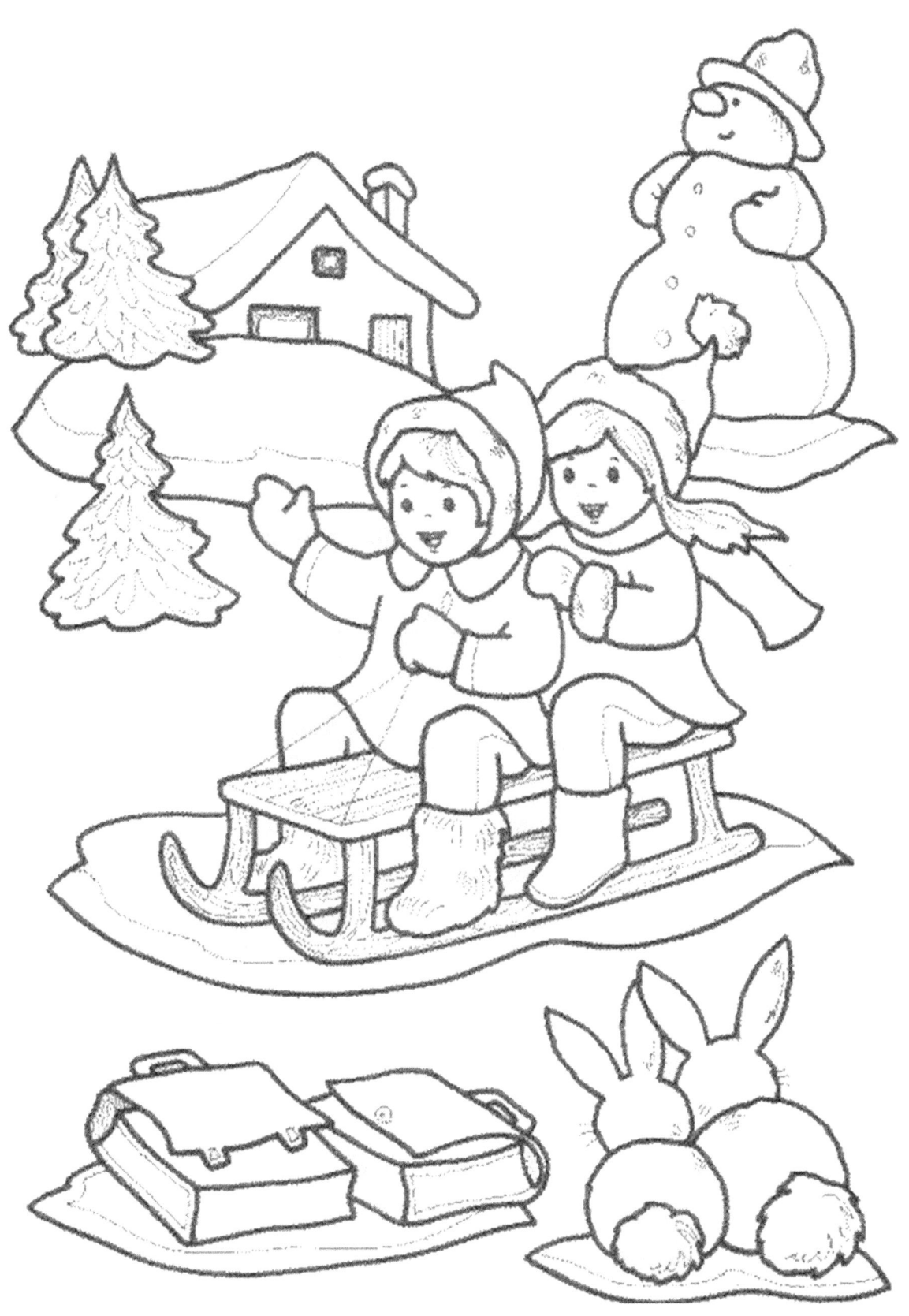

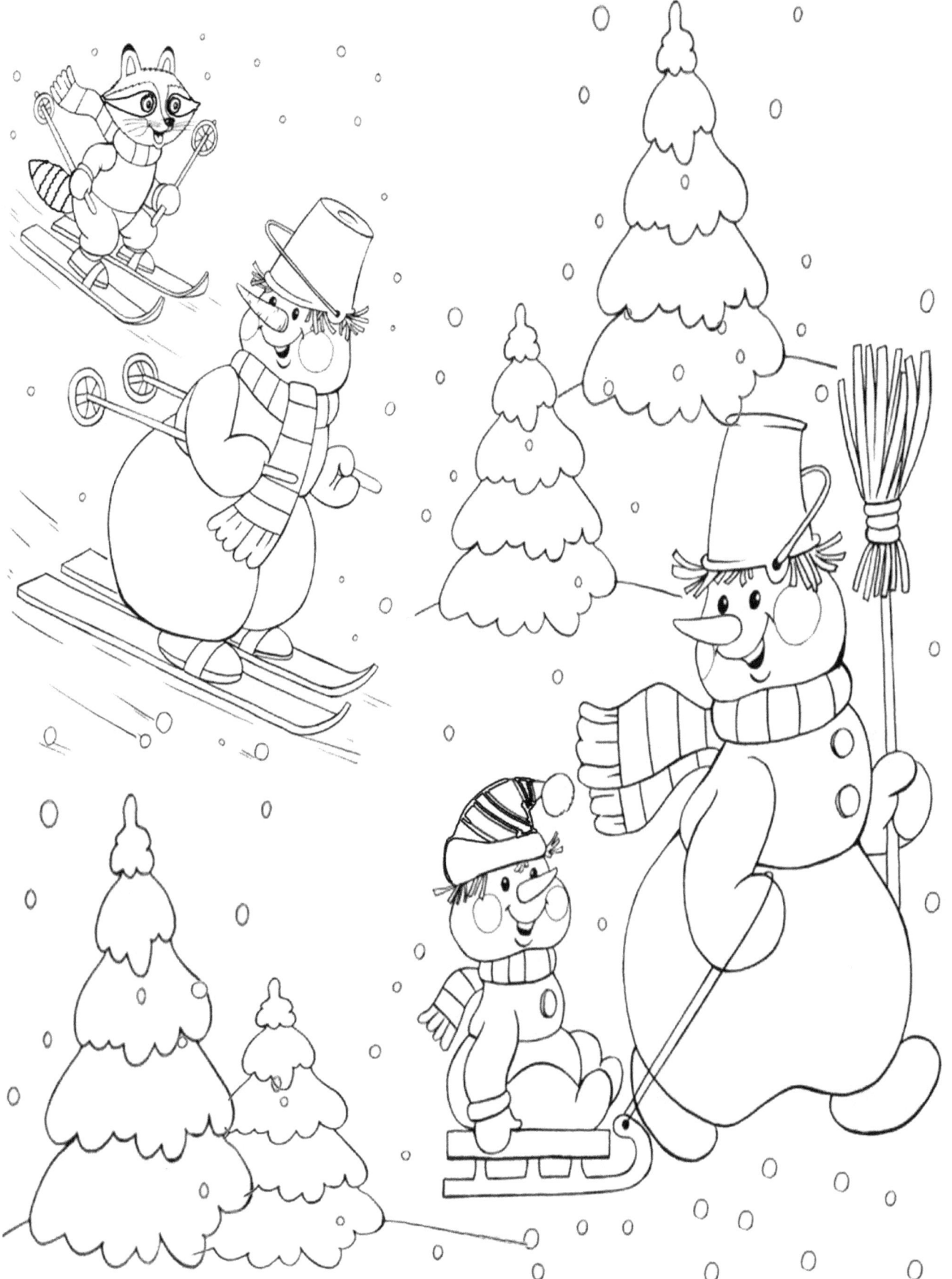

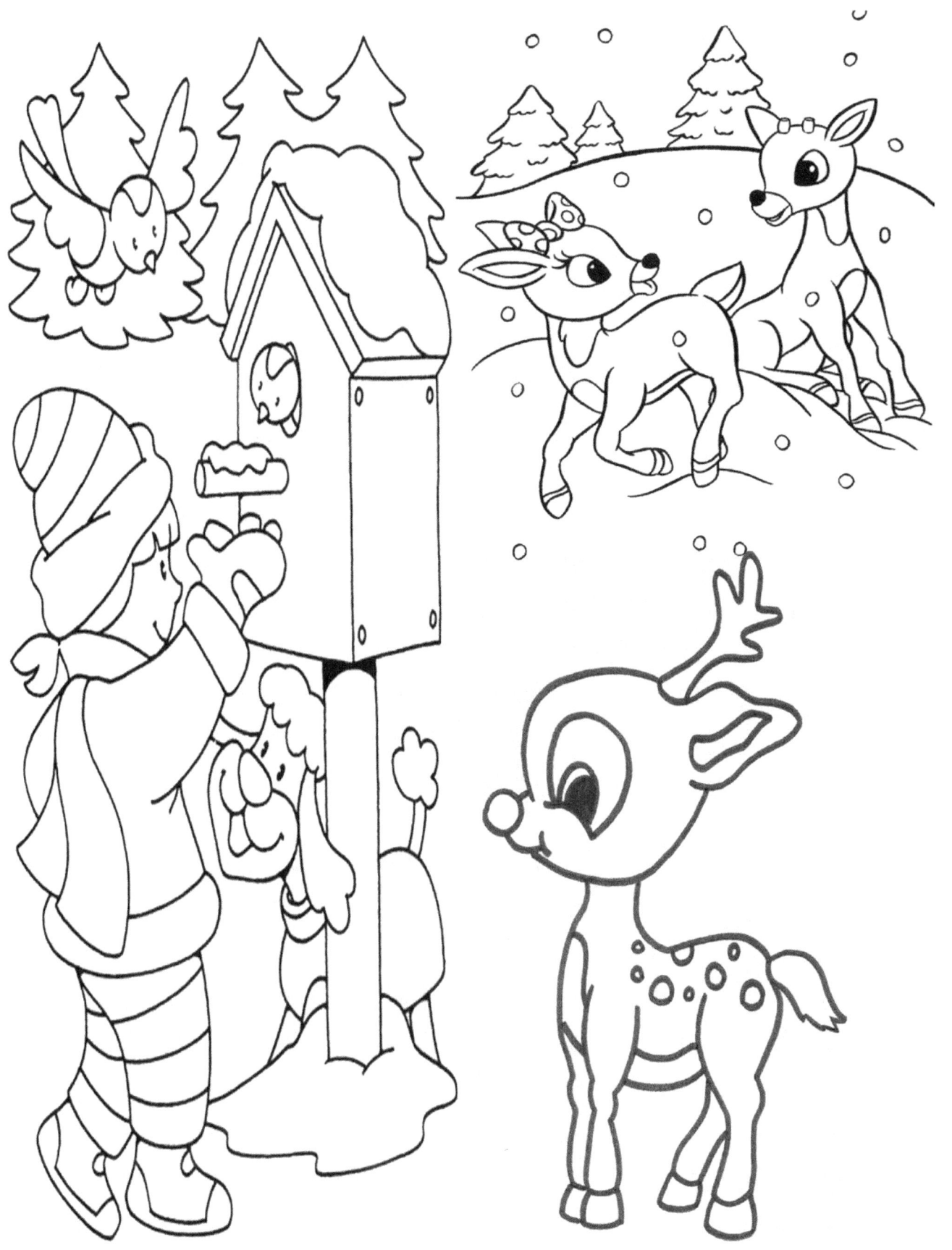

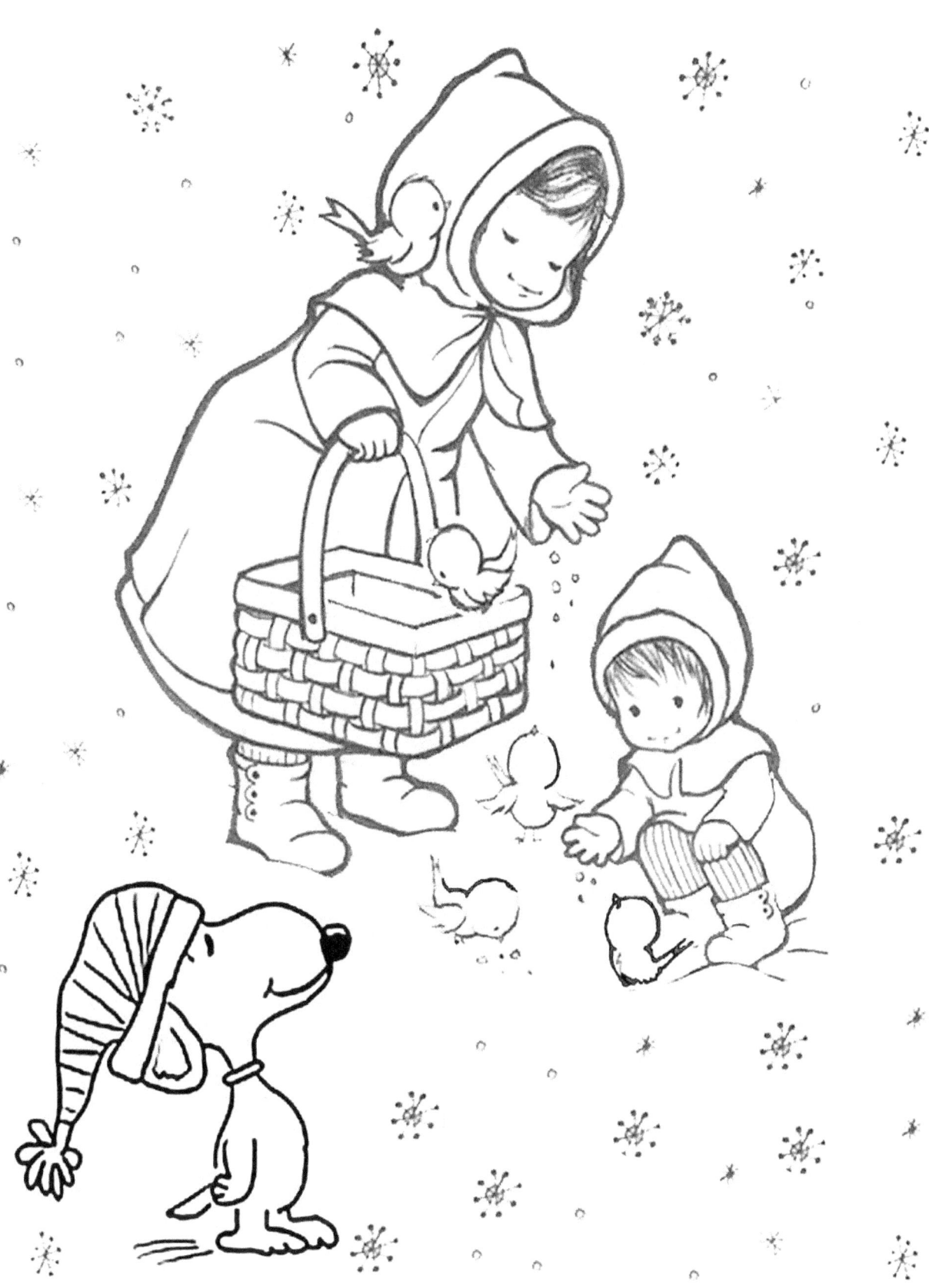

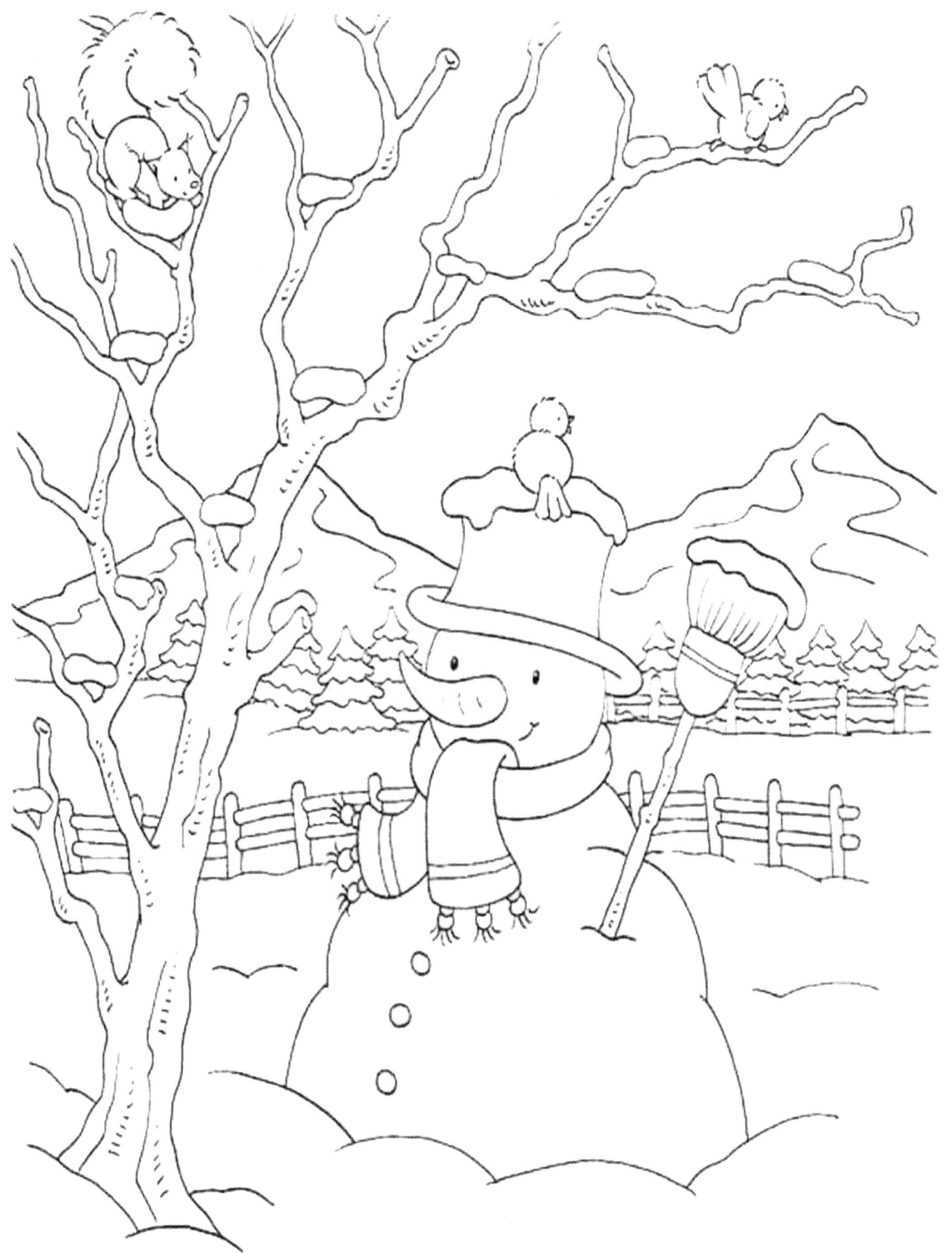

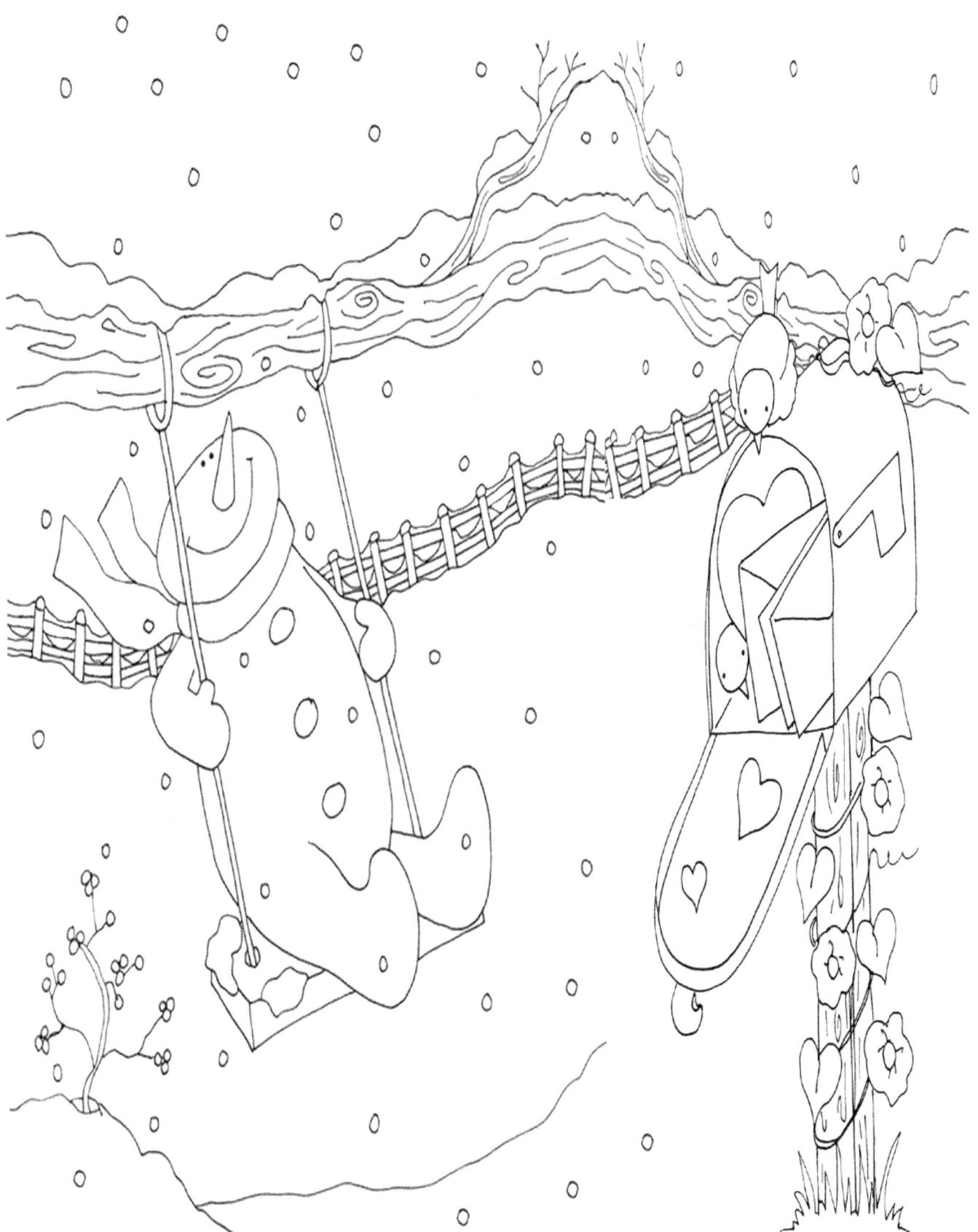

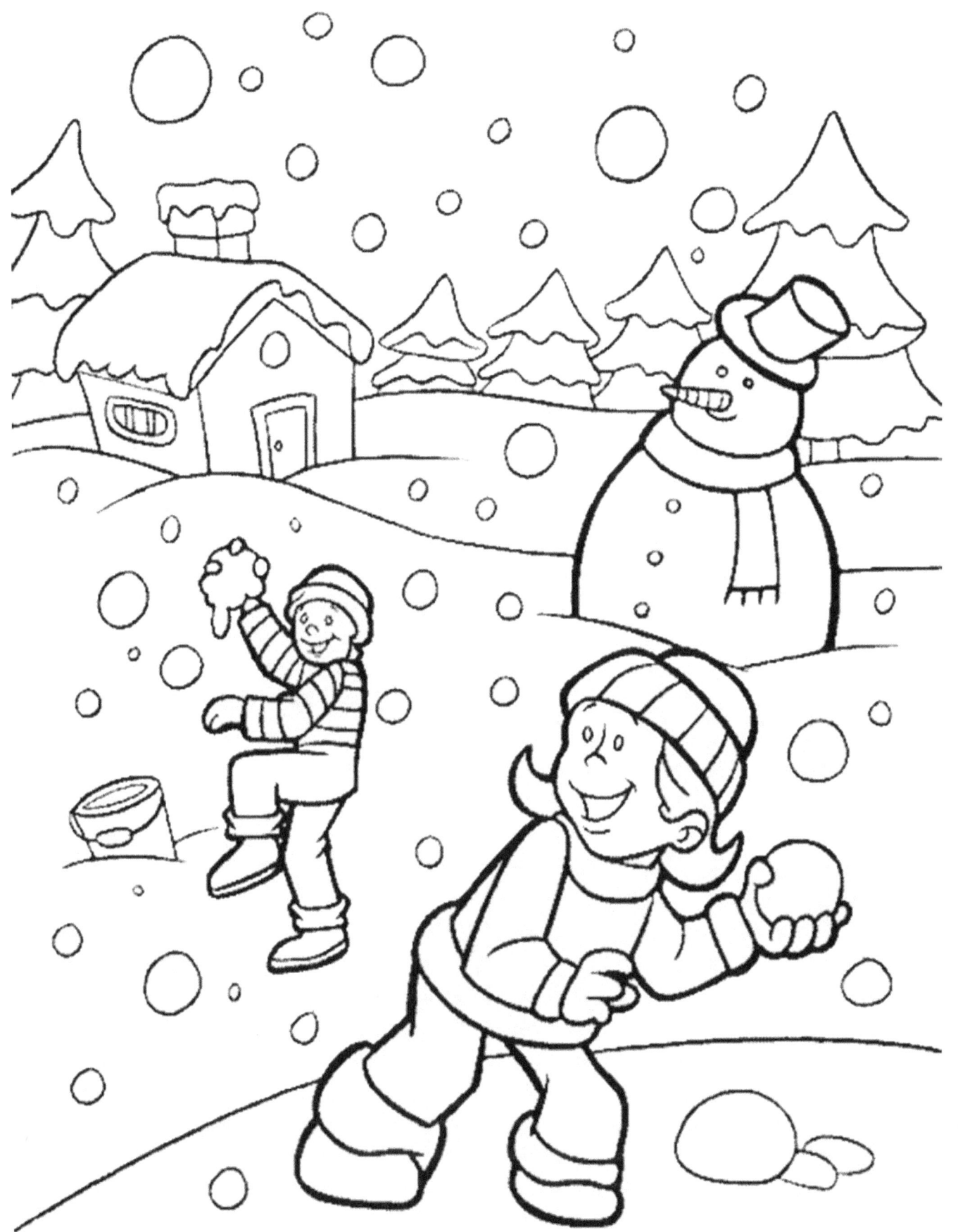

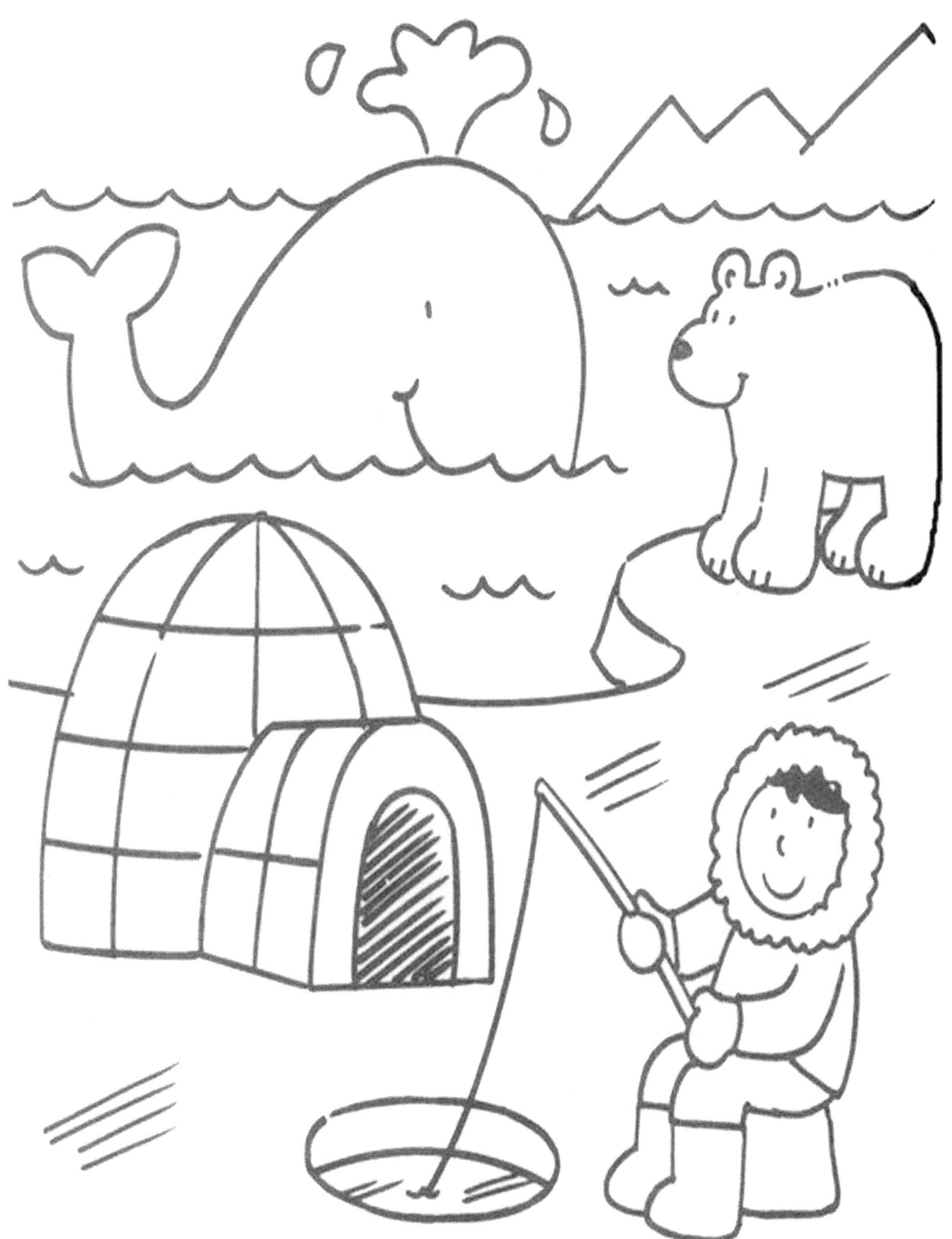

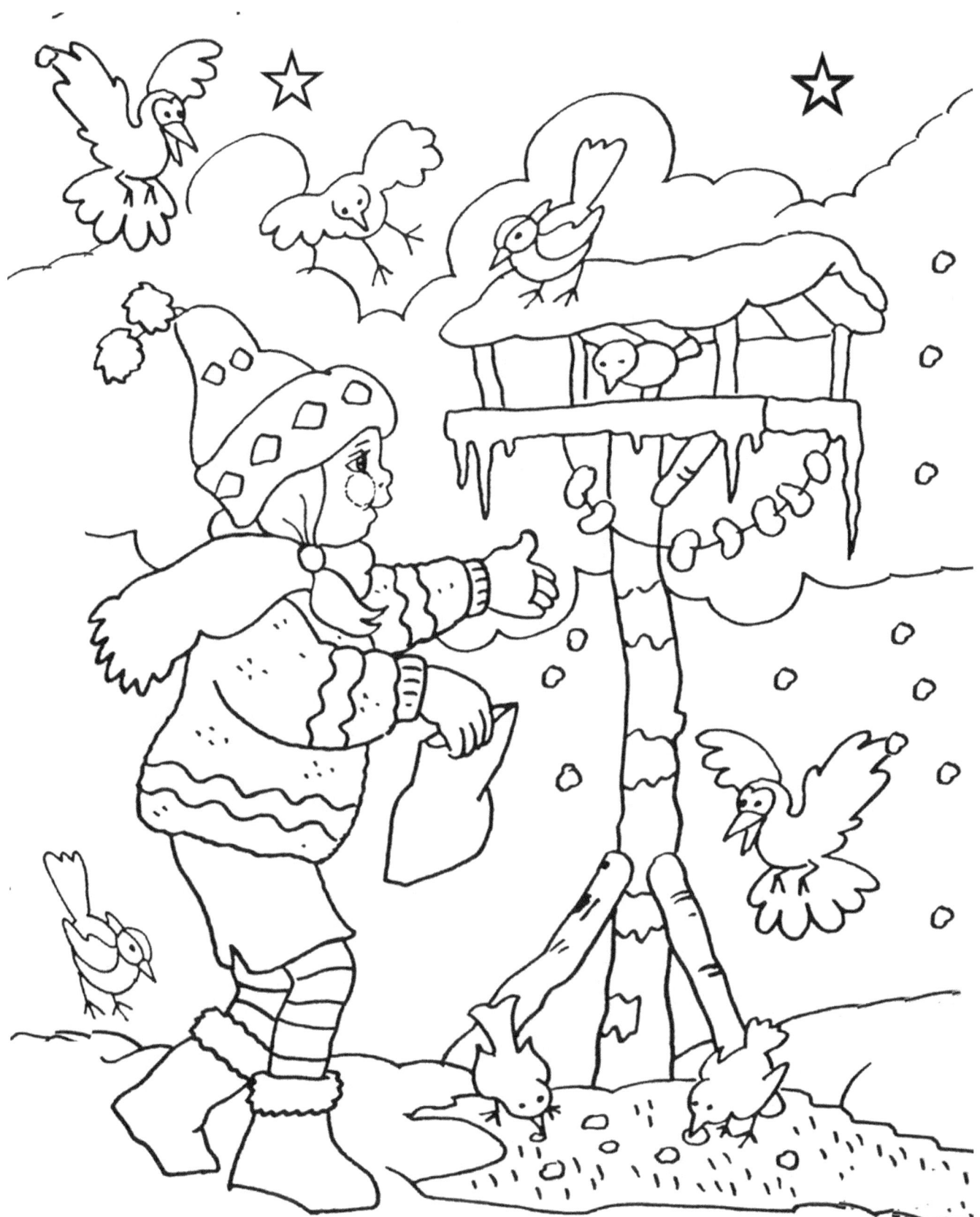

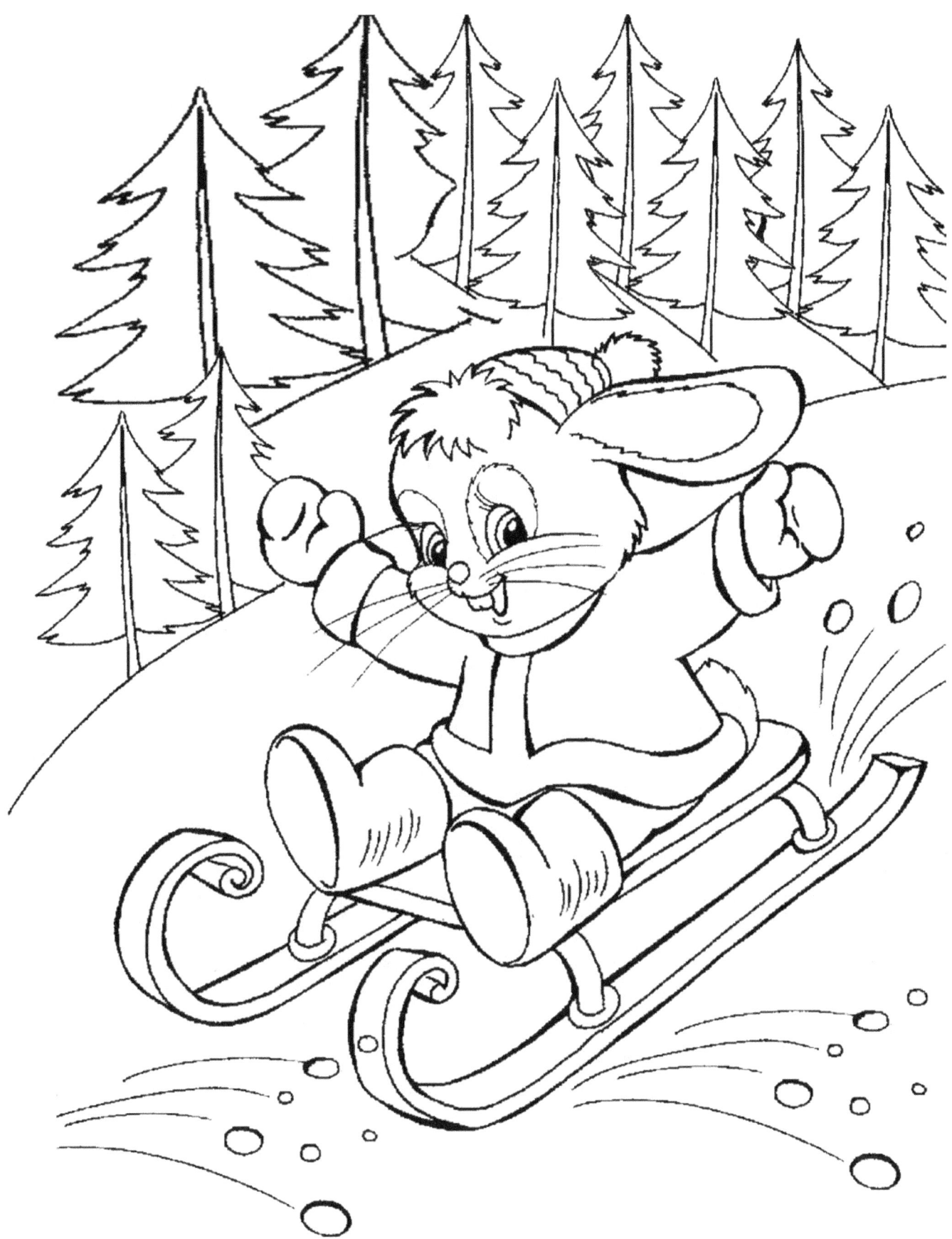

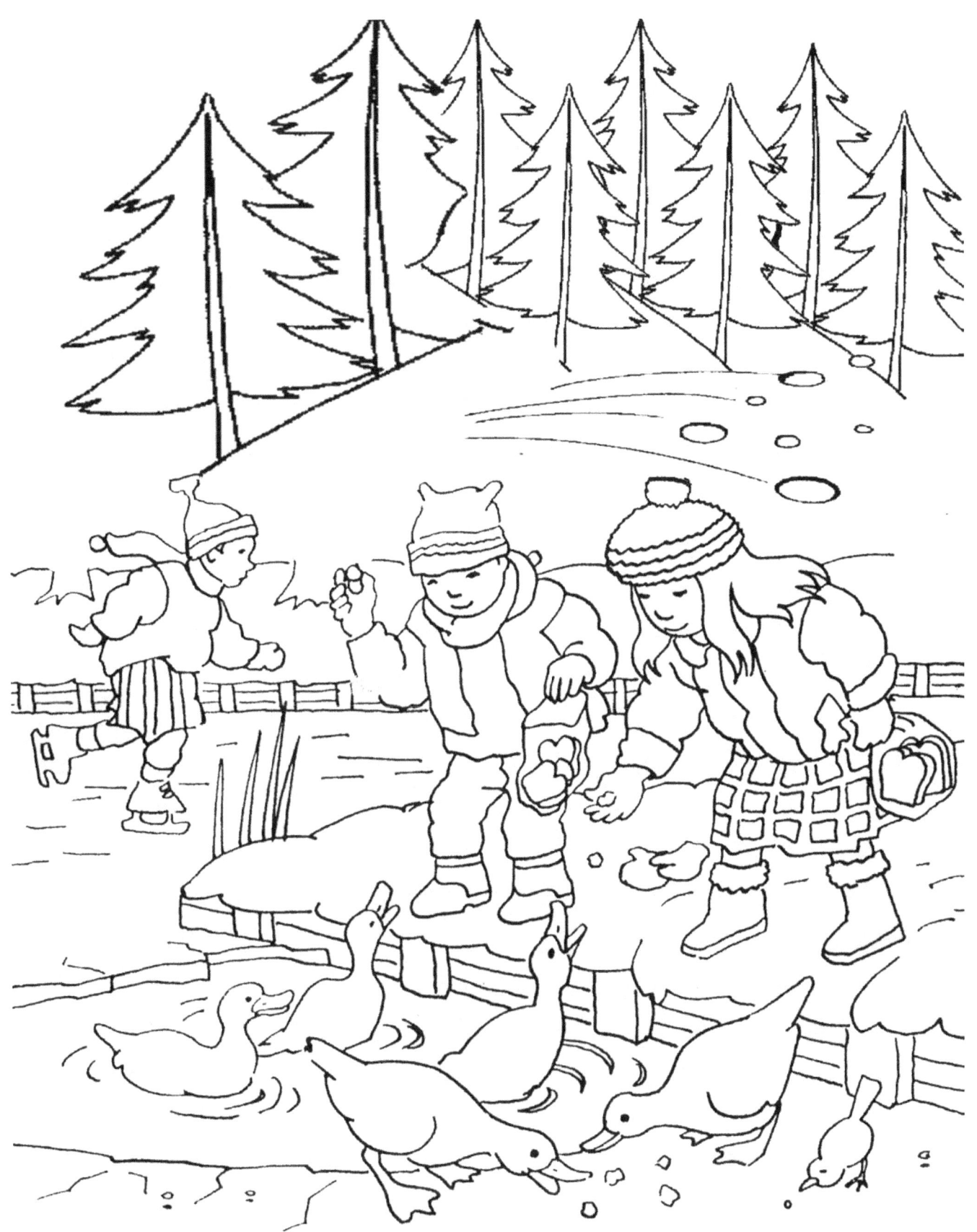

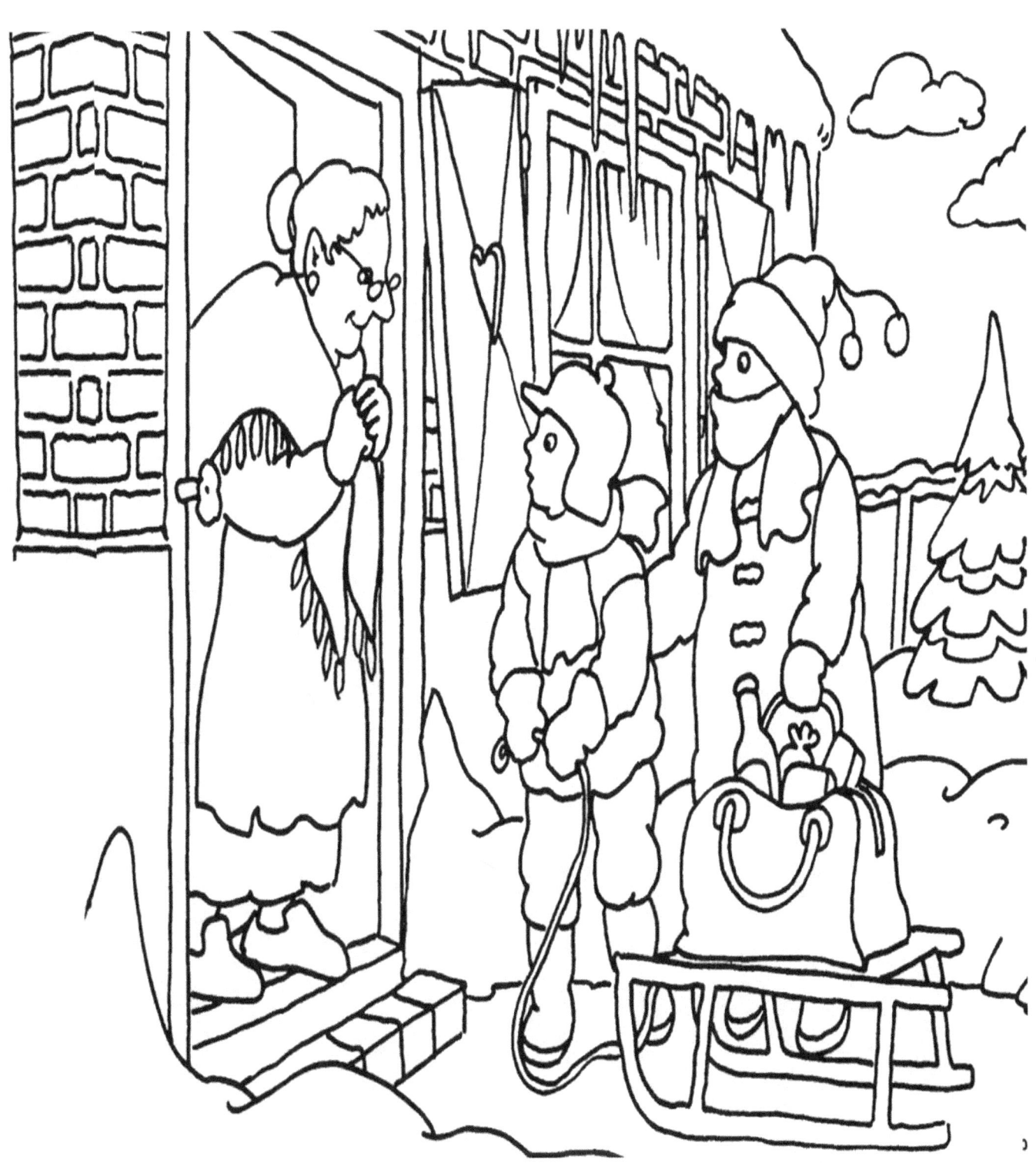

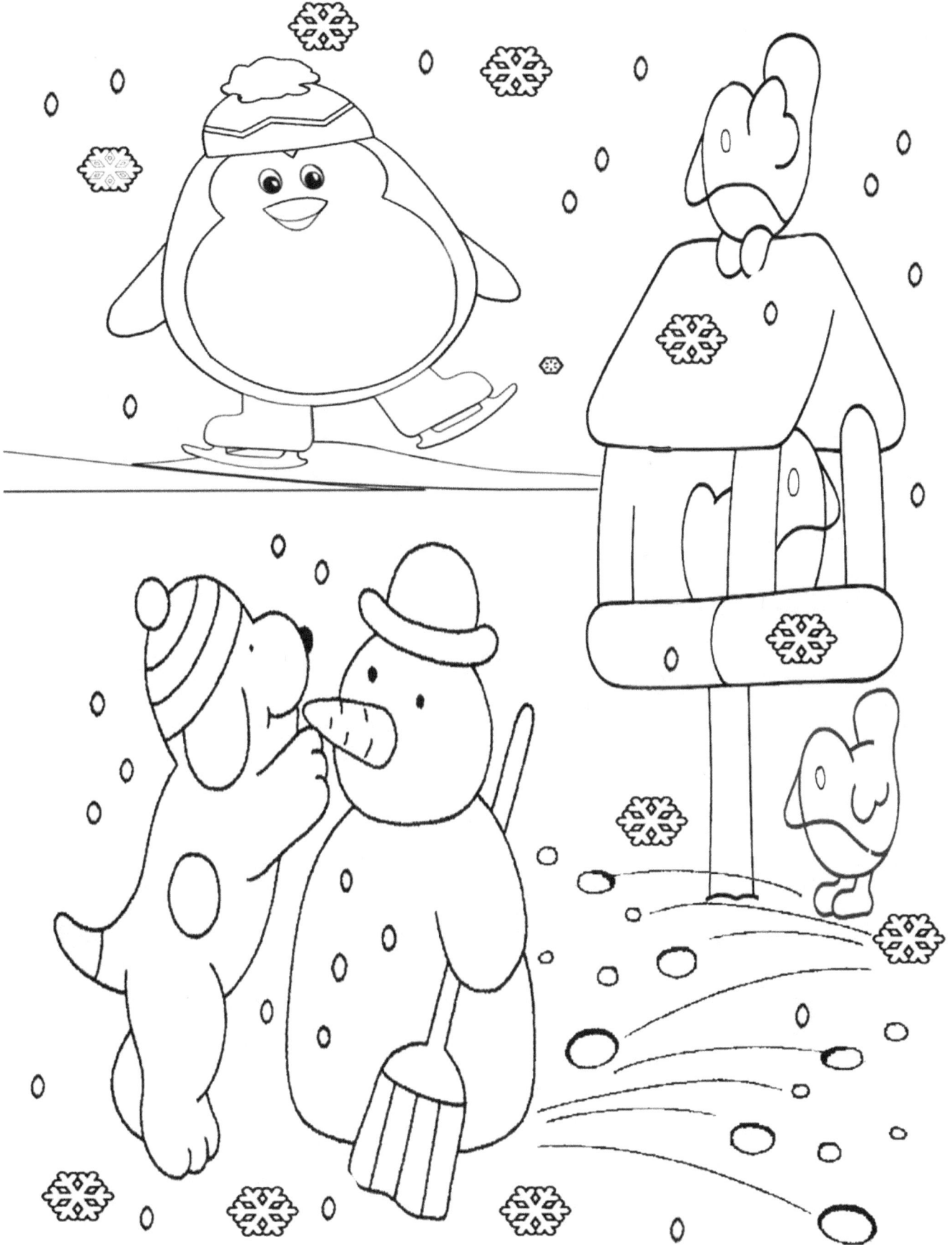

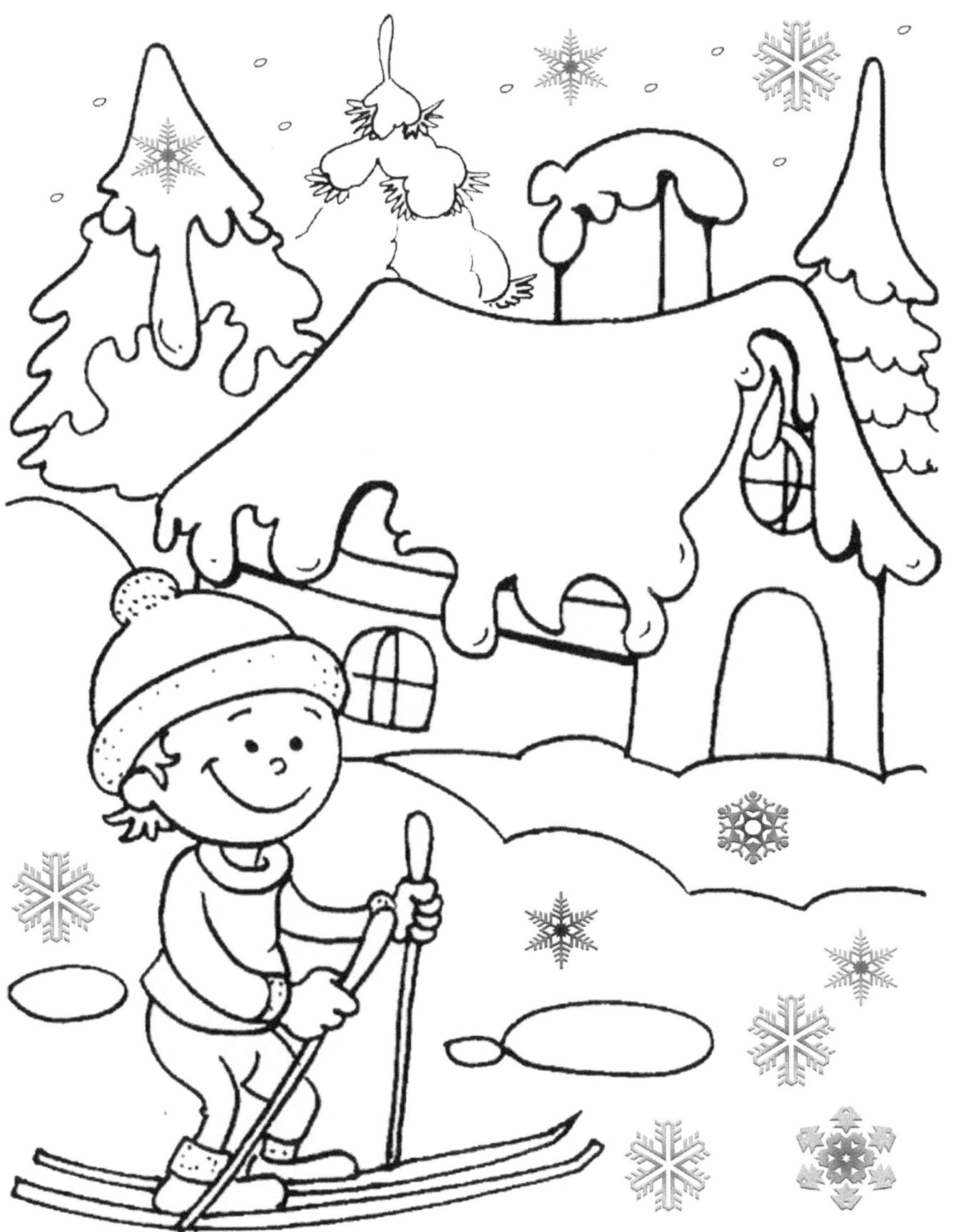

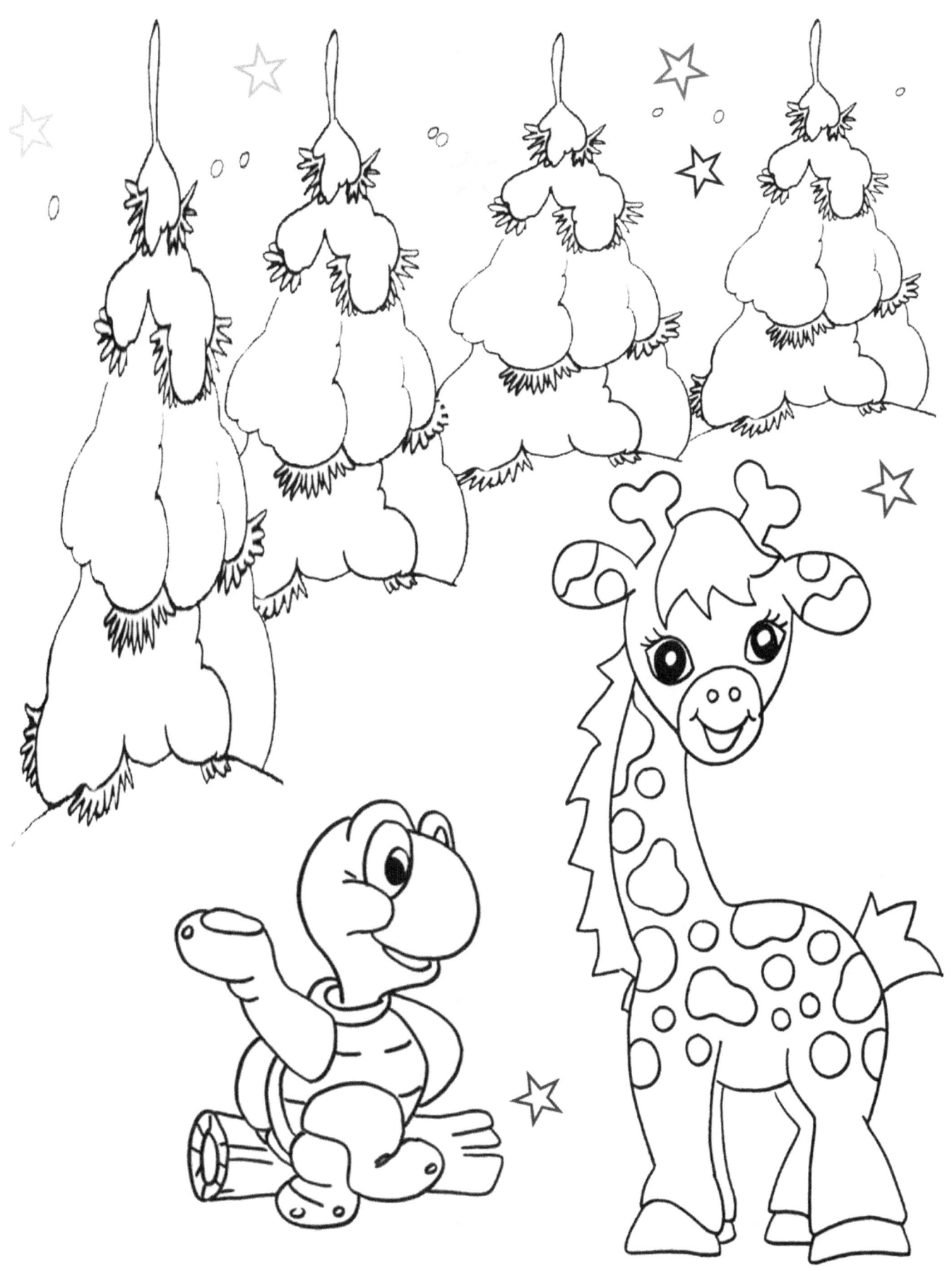

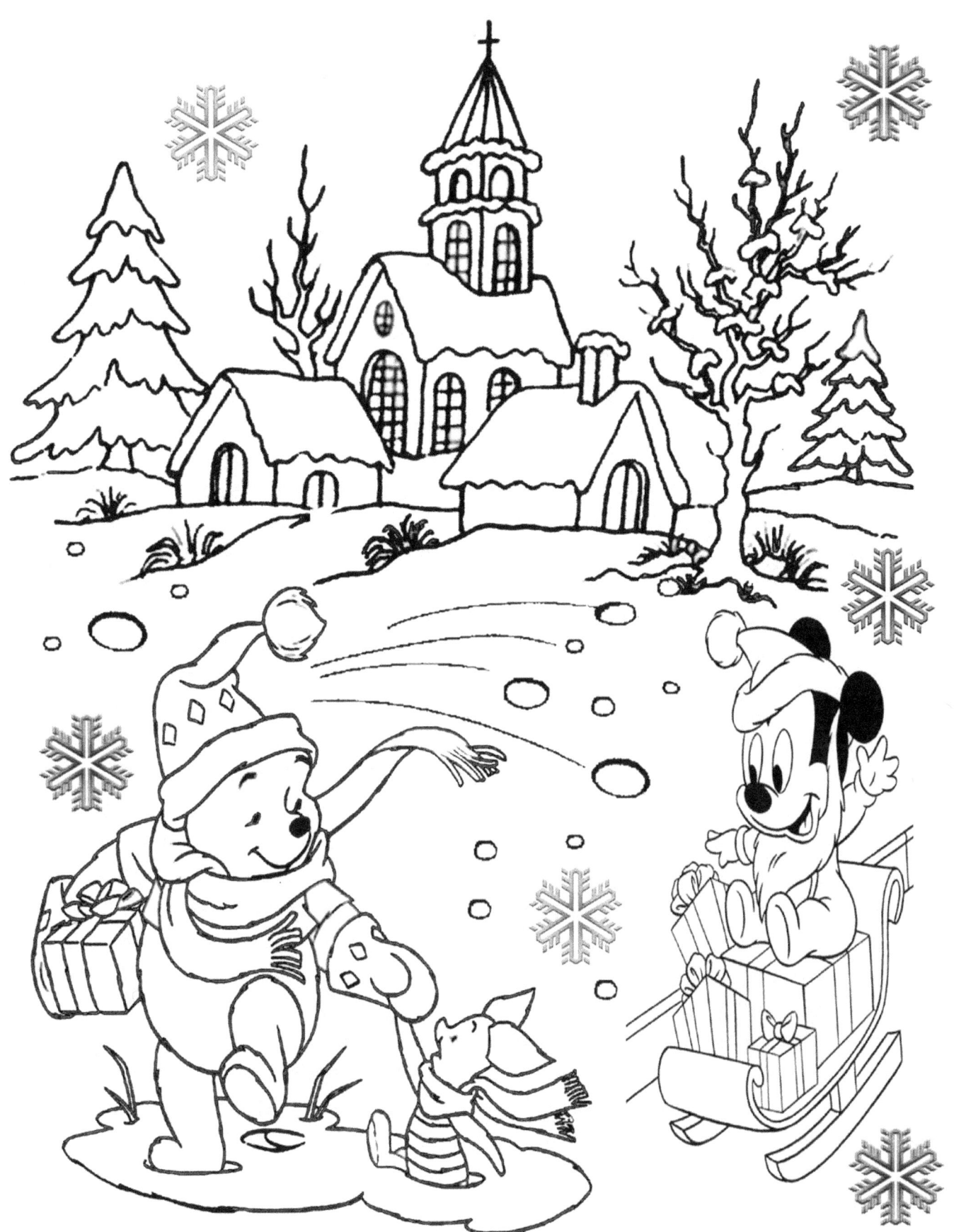

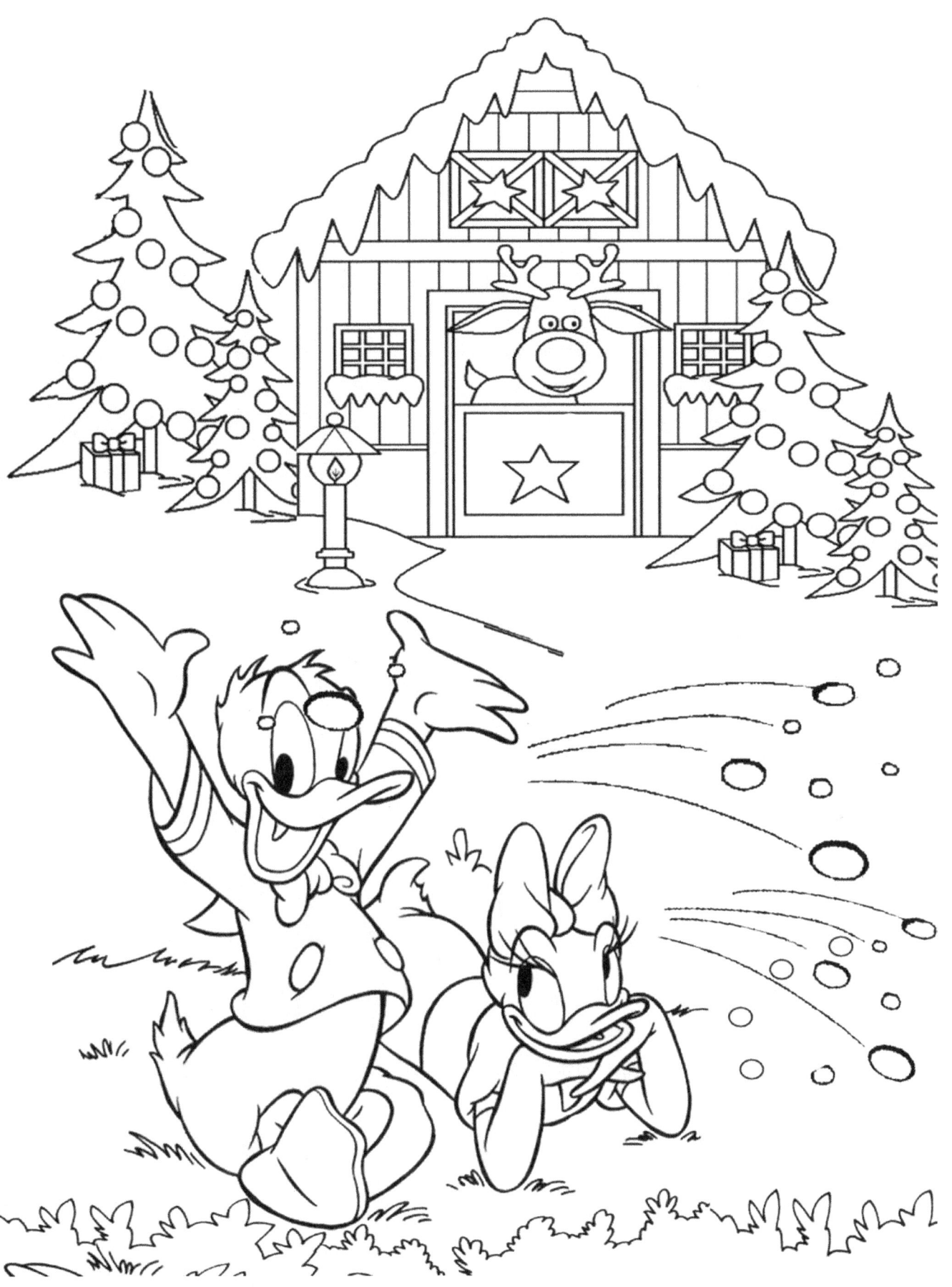

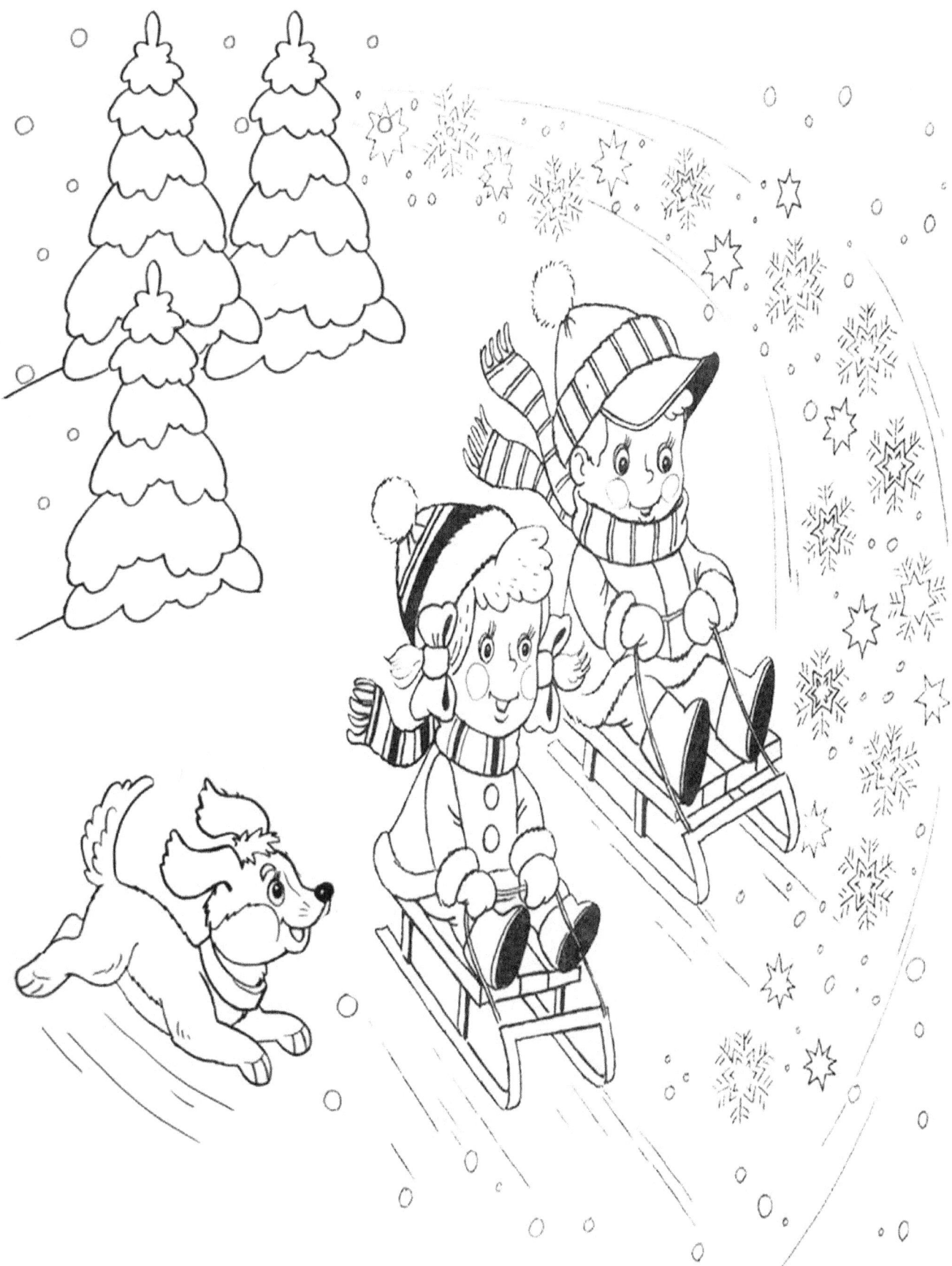

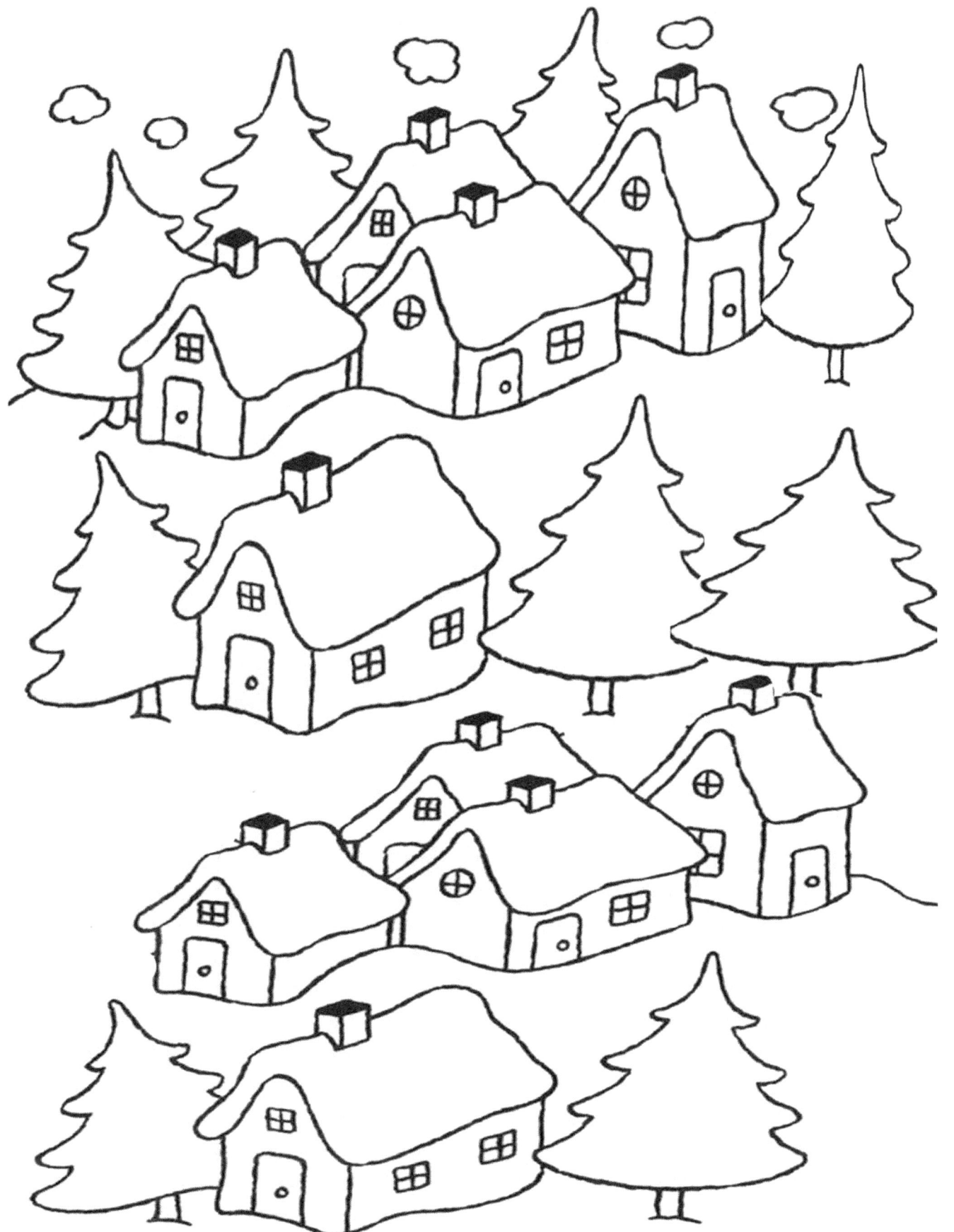

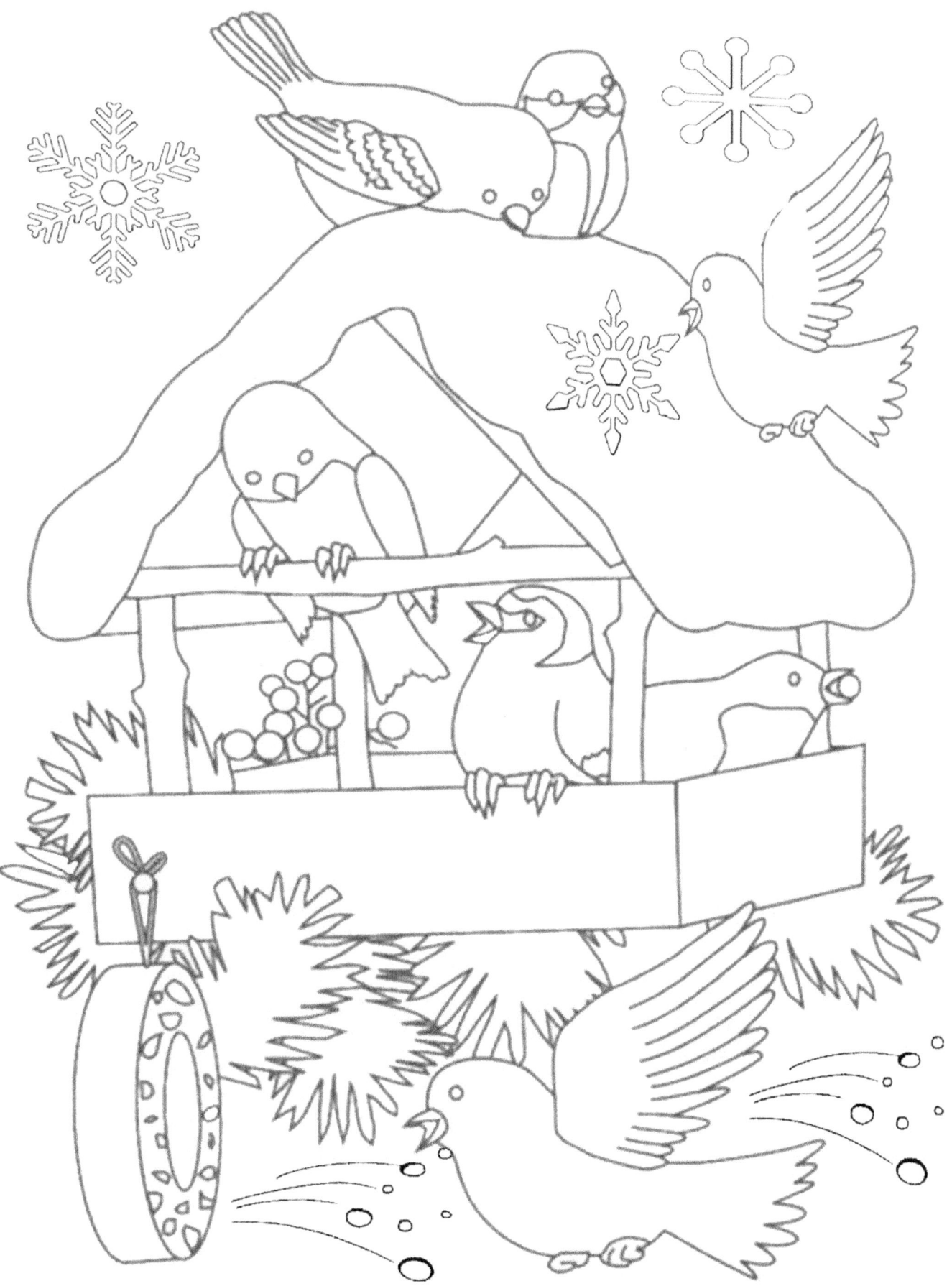

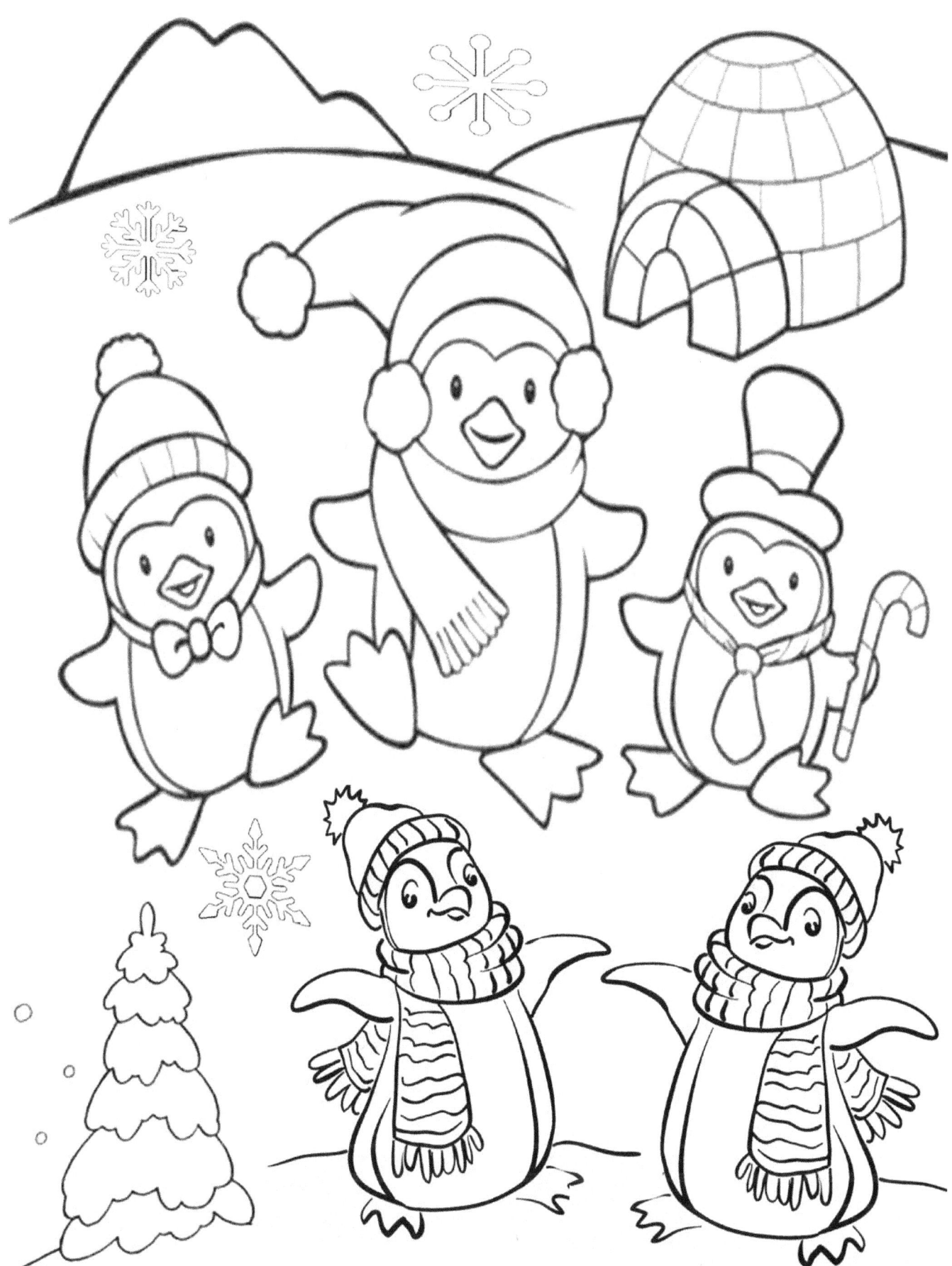

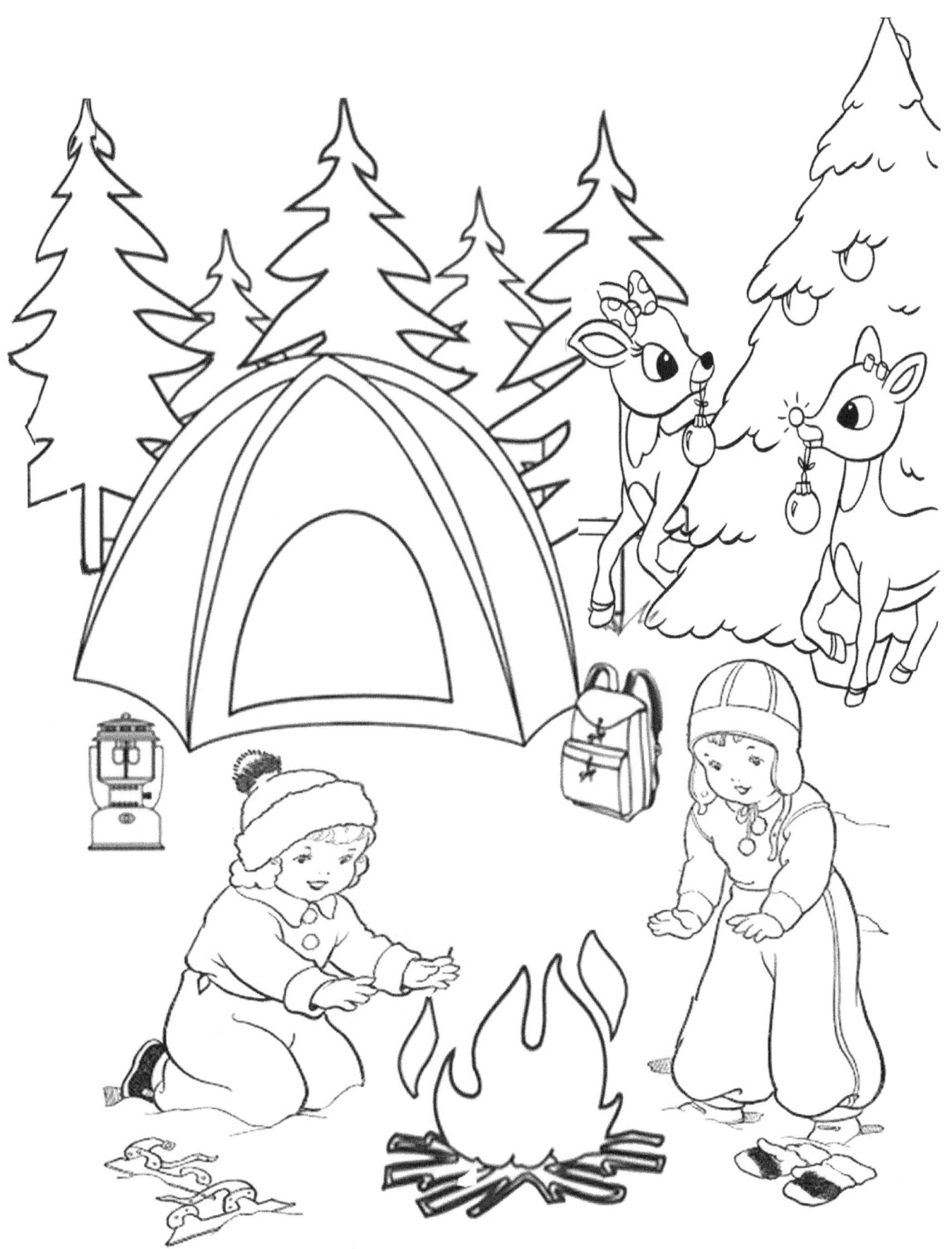

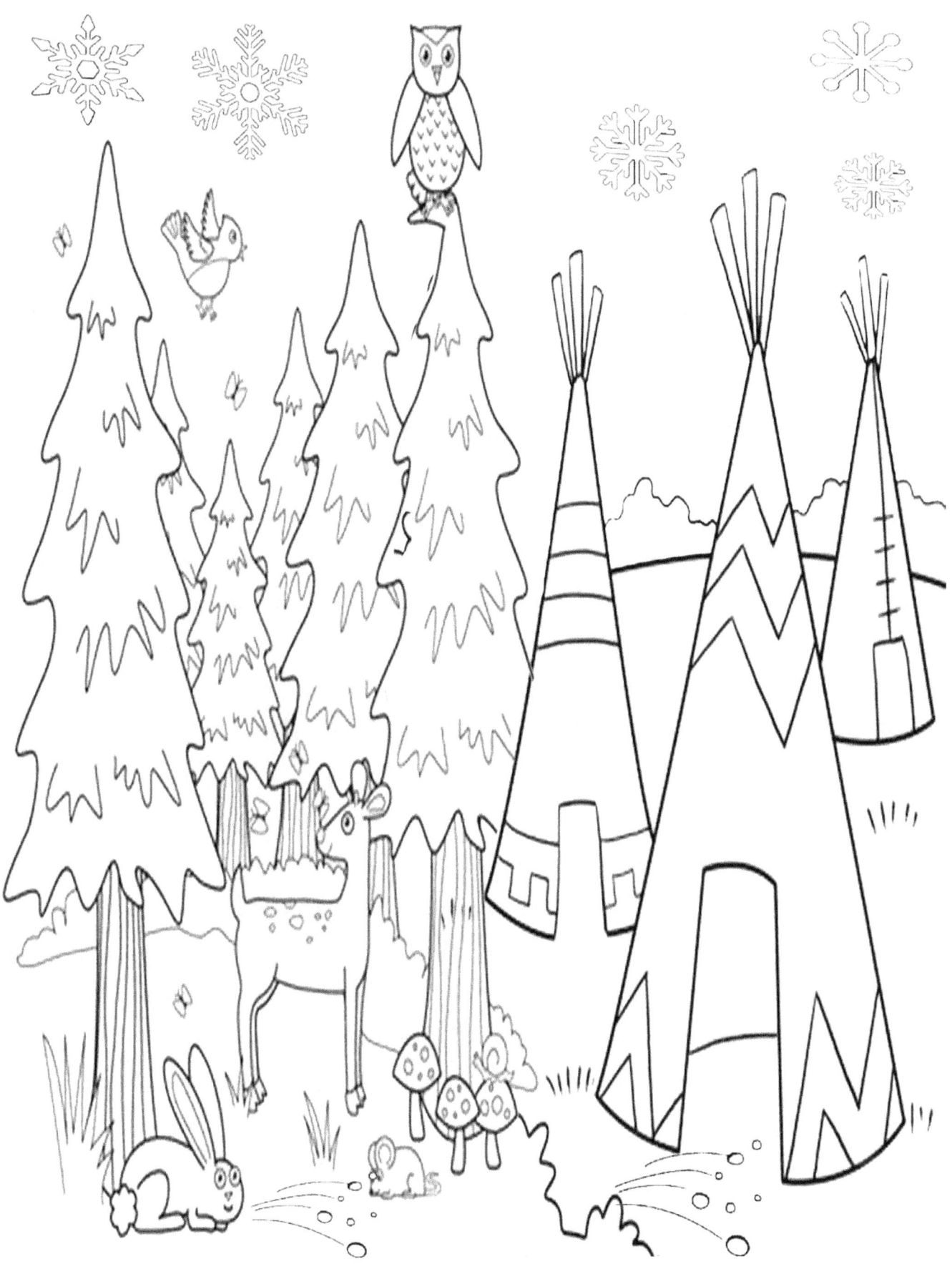

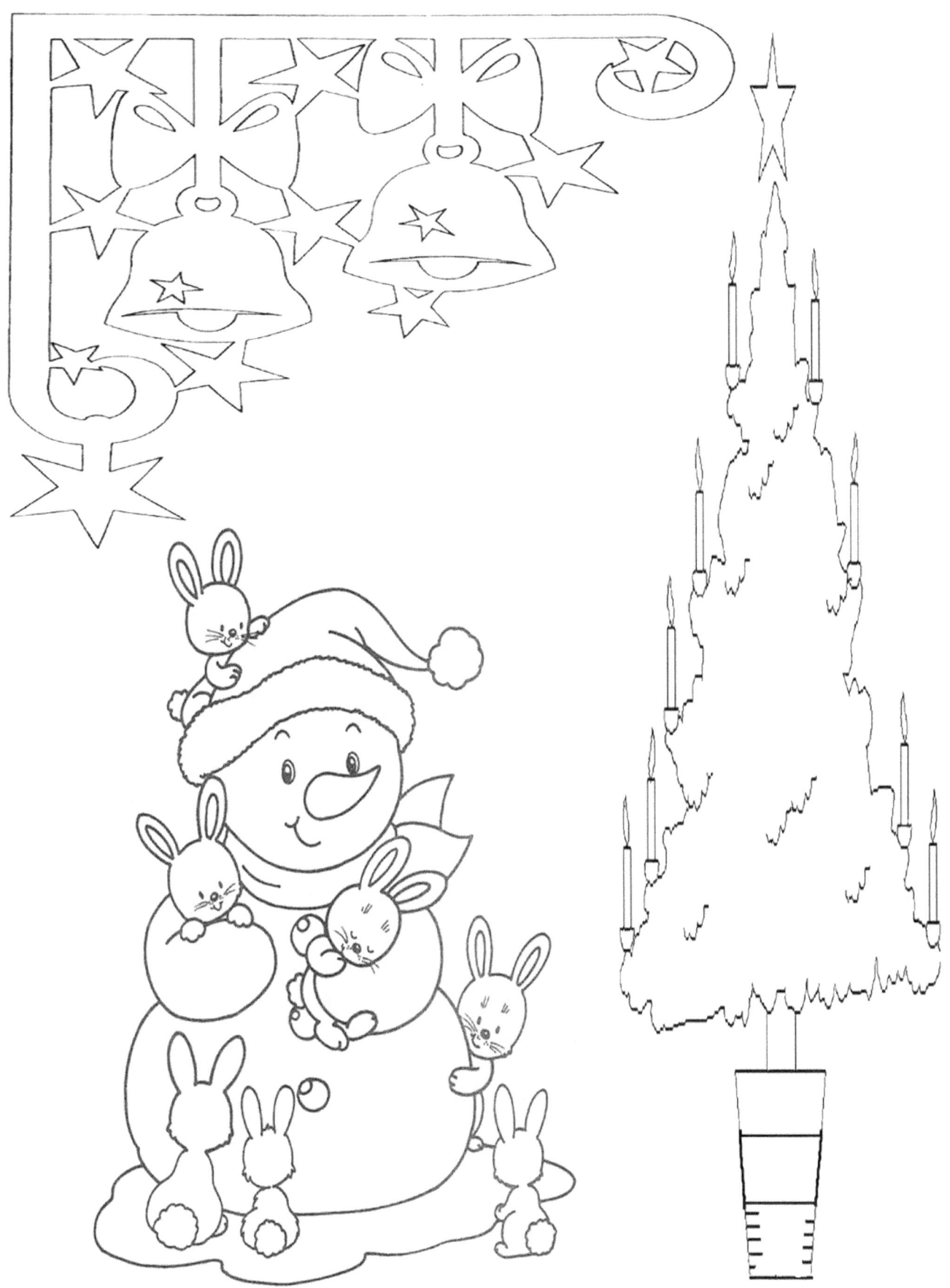

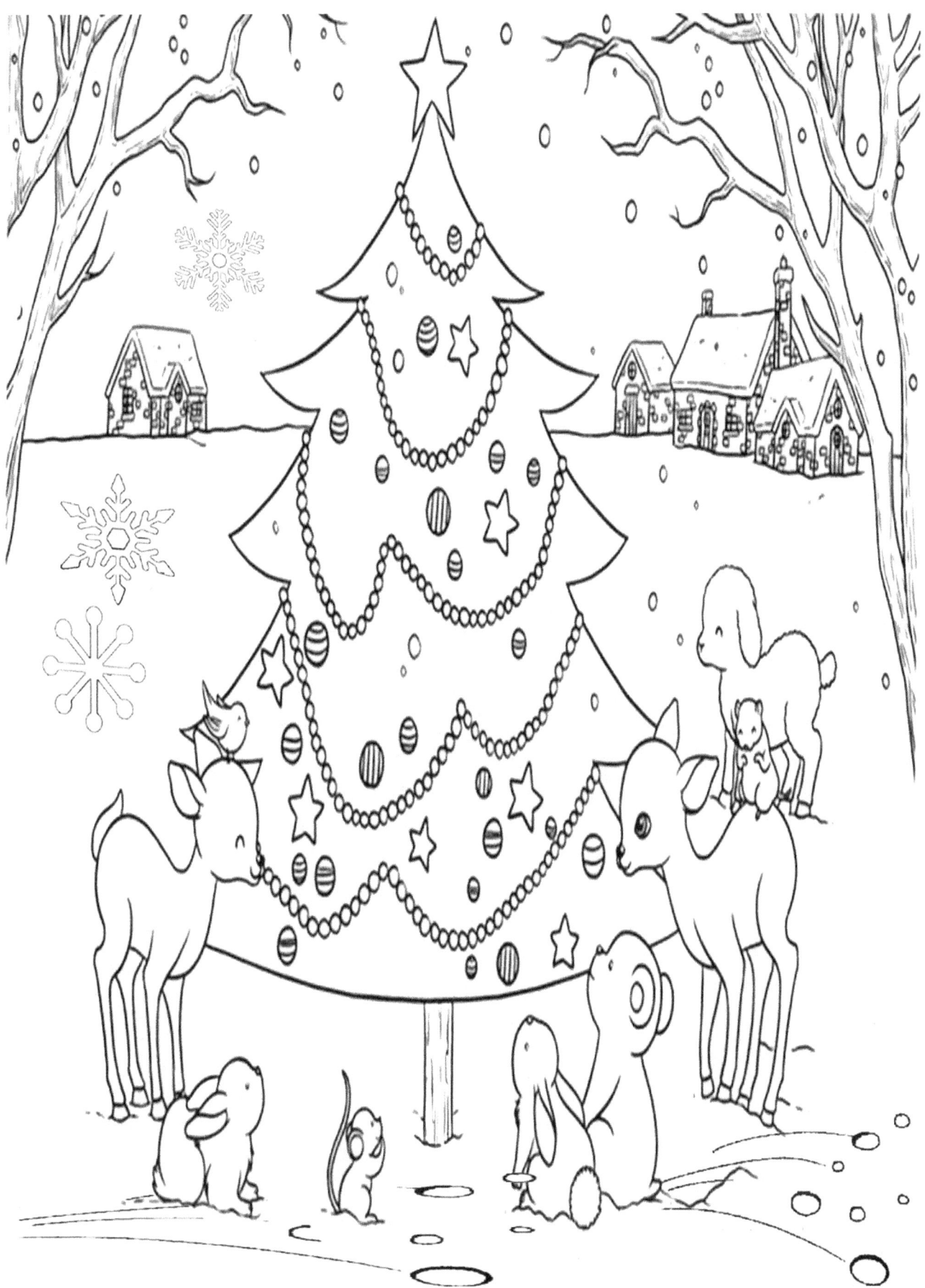

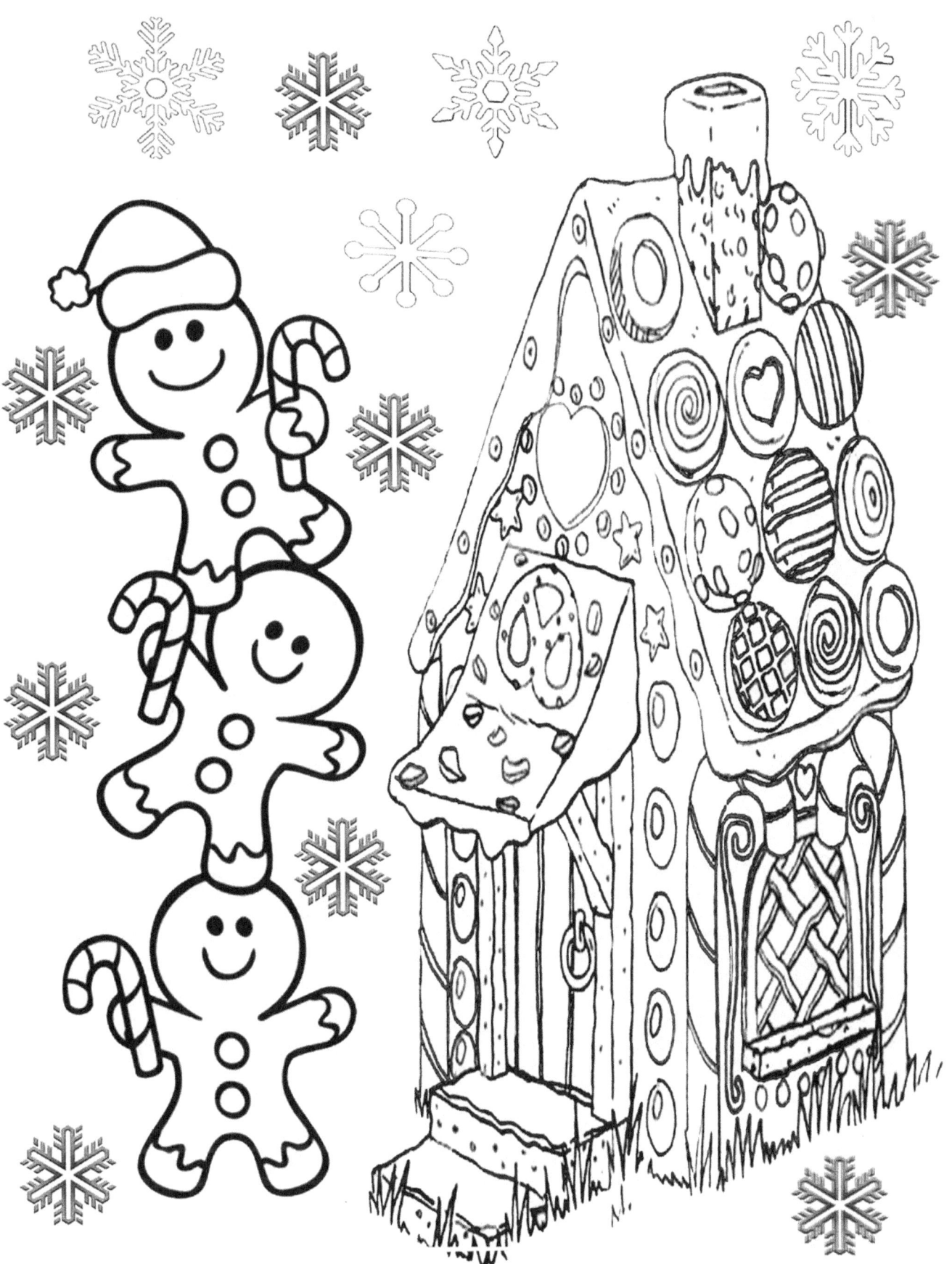

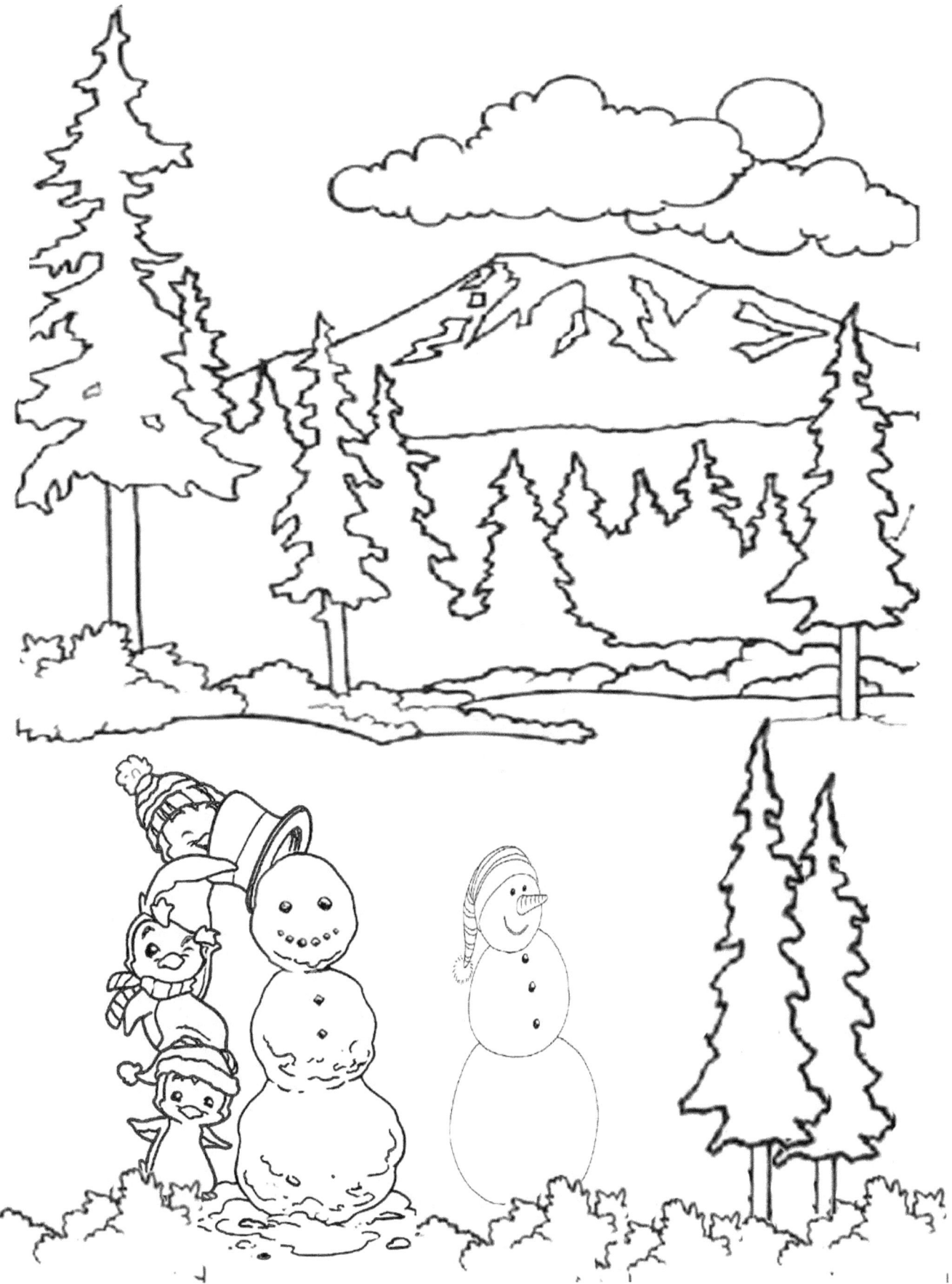

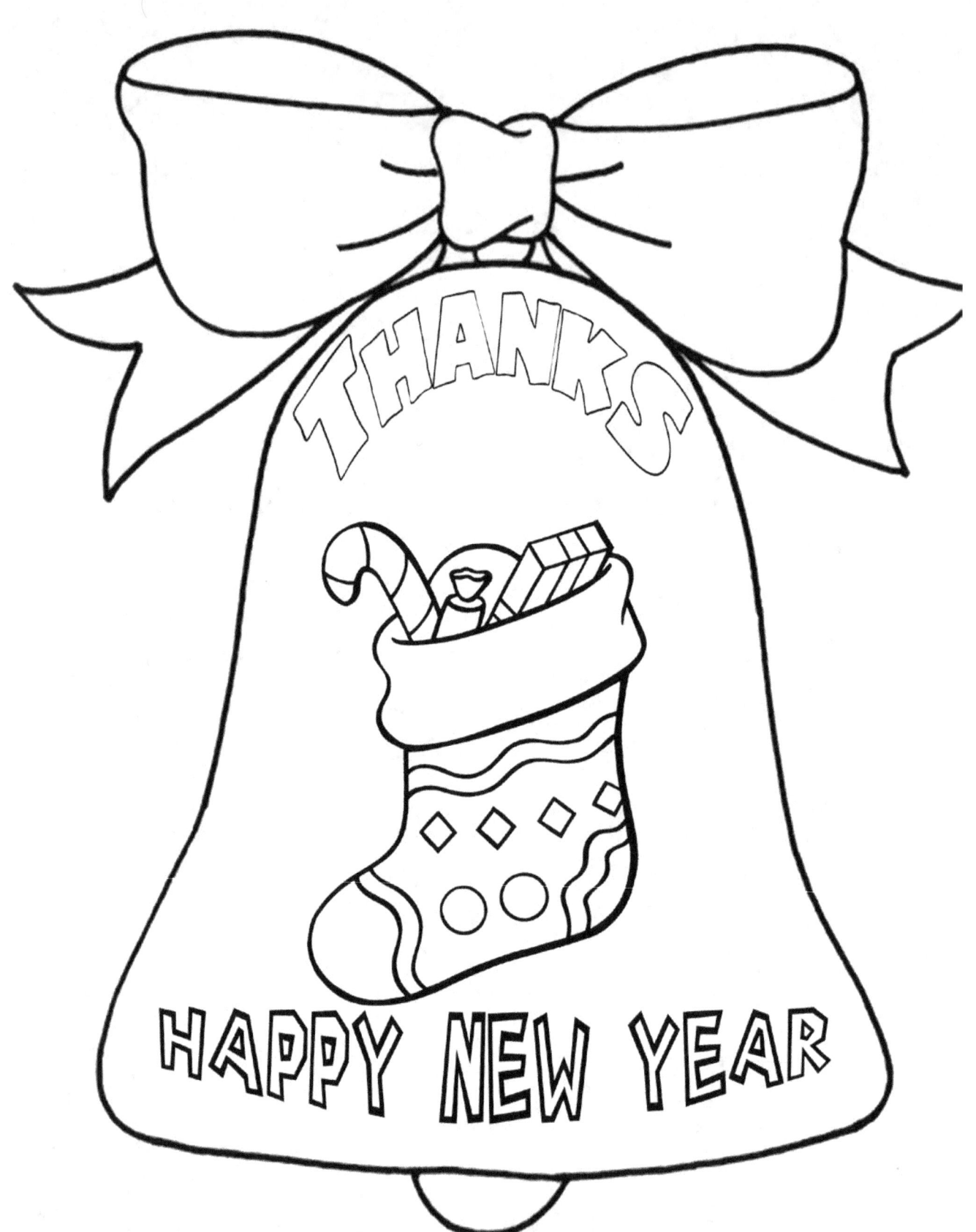

www.ingramcontent.com/pod-product-compliance
Lightning Source LLC
Chambersburg PA
CBHW060001230526
45472CB00008B/1896